Beyond Doubt

FAITH-BUILDING DEVOTIONS
ON QUESTIONS CHRISTIANS ASK

Cornelius Plantinga Jr.

William B. Eerdmans Publishing Company

Grand Rapids, Michigan / Cambridge, U.K.

Wm. B. Eerdmans Publishing Co.
255 Jefferson Ave. S.E., Grand Rapids, Michigan 49503 /
P.O. Box 163, Cambridge CB3 9PU U.K.
www.eerdmans.com

Printed in the United States of America

07 06 05 04 03   7 6 5 4 3 2

ISBN 0-8028-4965-2

Unless otherwise noted, the Scripture quotations in this publication
are from the New Revised Standard Version of the Bible, copyright ©
1989 by the Division of Christian Education of the National Council
of Churches of Christ in the U.S.A., and used by permission.

This book is a revised edition of material that previously appeared in
Beyond Doubt: A Devotional Response to Questions of Faith, published
by CRC Publications in 1980 and in *Assurances of the Heart: Faith-
Building Devotions on Questions Christians Ask,* published by Zondervan Publishing House in 1993.

Beyond Doubt

Contents

Contents

Contents

Questions about the Church

Questions about the Last Things

Contents

Introduction

Beyond Doubt began life as a manual for adult education classes in the church. In 1978 my denomination, the Christian Reformed Church in North America, asked me to write a book of Christian doctrine that could be taken in small doses. So I wrote meditations, the church added a Leader's Guide, and the result was published in 1980. Thirteen years later Zondervan republished the meditations alone under the title *Assurances of the Heart*.

I'm delighted, now, to introduce the Eerdmans edition. To prepare it, I've written a number of new meditations and trimmed up the others, usually by pruning overgrown sentences and choosing fresh illustrations. In addition, I've replaced many of my own prayers with better ones from the Psalms.

Beyond Doubt is a devotional that raises questions about the Christian faith and then addresses them in groups of five meditations. Some of the questions are old and basic: What is God like? What did Jesus do? If the Lord is with us, why do we suffer? Some questions are practical: How should we Christians see ourselves? Why pray? How should we handle our wealth? All, I believe, are real questions that real Christians ask.

The idea throughout the 135 meditations is to *address* these questions. I don't always answer them, at least not completely. Some of them are too big and hard for any human being to answer fully —

even one who is instructed by Scripture. But some questions invite straightforward answers, and where this is the case I offer them. The point either way is to help believers reflect on these questions, see into them more deeply, ponder some answers, and do all of this in a way that strengthens faith.

The meditations in this book do reflect contemporary Christian experience in North America. At the same time, I have used traditional theological structure (the volume begins with God and ends with the last things) and have tried to exercise firm biblical control throughout. The result is a hybrid — neither a collection of miscellaneous pieces nor a short systematic theology, but rather a book of existential devotions with a theological spine.

The style is meant to be plain but not graceless. If readers detect seepage from my reading of good children's literature, I would be pleased. Two other usage notes: I refer to God with masculine pronouns and titles, not because I think God is male (I don't), but simply to follow prevailing scriptural usage. Second, in referring to human beings I alternate the use of masculine and feminine pronouns in an attempt to be inclusive without awkwardly repeating "he or she," "his or her," and so forth.

I'd like to acknowledge the help of my associate at Calvin College, Sue A. Rozeboom, who read and commented on the whole manuscript, and also the encouragement of Jon Pott, Editor-in-Chief at Eerdmans and a wonderful friend.

These meditations are inspired in tone and content by the preaching of Douglas E. Nelson (1913-89), minister for more than two decades of the First Presbyterian Church of New Haven, Connecticut, and my mentor for many years. Doug's thoughts, phrases, stories, and examples are liberally scattered through these meditations — often, but not always, with acknowledgment. He kindly granted me this freedom, and, after he died, Doug's wife, Jerry, graciously renewed it.

For many of us Christians there are, beyond our parents, two or three people who truly form our lives. They bring Christ to us. Douglas E. Nelson was such a person for me. Beneath the sheen on Doug's sermons was the texture of understanding in them, the almost desperately deep fathoming of human trouble and divine grace, and of the surprising places they intersect. Doug taught me that no honest question is ever out of place in a Christian life and that a Christian faith that asks questions is often stronger than a faith that asks nothing.

To Doug I dedicate this book with love and respect.

CORNELIUS PLANTINGA JR.

Questions about God

Question 1

How Do We Come to Know God?

The most important question in the world is the question about God. Are we human beings alone in the cosmos? Are we, so to speak, as good as it gets in the universe of intelligent creatures? Or are we at this very moment in the unspeakable presence of One who is both a terror and a joy, at once an enemy of evil and an overflowing fountain of goodness? How do we know?

Believers ask in order to deepen their belief. Believers in God do not step out of their skin and pretend to be skeptics. Instead, from inside their faith, believers ask big questions because the faith that knows God also wants to know God better. Faith seeks understanding, as St. Anselm said. So believers ask a primary question: How do we come to know God?

1

*The LORD said to me, "Assemble the people for me, and
I will let them hear my words, so that they may learn to
fear me as long as they live on the earth, and may teach
their children so."*

DEUTERONOMY 4:10

Many children come to know about God from their father or mother. Children learn about a sort of person named God. We can't see this person, but he can see us. And we can talk to him. God is great. God is good. God is extremely high. And he has a lot to do with another person by the name of Jesus. Either may be called "the Lord."

It's not long before children reflect on these things. Then they ask wonderful questions: How can God see us without eyes? What does God look like? Is God stronger than Superman? Is Jesus the same person as God? Parents do their best with such questions. Meanwhile, children notice that just as they are fastened to their parents by need and love, so their parents are fastened to God. Surprisingly, parents turn out, in a way, to be children too — children of God. This fact impresses youngsters. They notice that all the really basic parts of the Christian faith seem to come not *from* parents, but *through* them.

As children grow, they get worked into the family way of life. At the heart of it are attitudes and practices that tie the whole family to God. Taken together, these attitudes and practices are what we call religion. A main tie or bond in true religion is what the Bible calls "the fear of the LORD," which is an attitude of mixed reverence and love. A God-fearing person loves God with all his heart, but also feels tiny and unholy in the presence of God.

Parents try to teach their children this fear of the Lord. As today's Scripture shows, when parents teach their children to fear the Lord, those parents are themselves obedient children of God. Sometimes the fear of the Lord is not so much taught as caught. Children catch it from their parents' reverent tone of voice when they mention God. Children catch it when they glimpse their parents on their knees. When a child's mother says to her husband, "Greg, we can't *do* it! It simply isn't right!" the child perceives that this too has something to do with the fear of the Lord, even though the Lord hasn't been mentioned.

So it goes in untold numbers of families down the ages. We can see it beginning among the Israelites. They *learn* to fear the Lord so that they "may teach their children so."

> *God our Lord, we know you are kind and good. Yet let us reverently fear you for your power and holiness. We know you are strong and holy. Yet let us love you for your kindness and goodness. In Jesus' name, Amen.*

How Do We Come to Know God?

2

God also said to Moses, . . . "Go and assemble the elders
of Israel, and say to them, 'The LORD, *the God of your*
ancestors, the God of Abraham, of Isaac, and of Jacob,
has appeared to me, saying: I have given heed to you
and to what has been done to you in Egypt. I declare
that I will bring you up out of the misery of Egypt.'"

EXODUS 3:15-17

We come to know God through his Word. Already as children we may
have heard stories about God's great deeds and great love. Even with
today's busy schedules, many Christian families read the Bible at meal
time. Some read a Bible story before going to bed. Many of these readings reveal that God rescues his children. Most are interesting. Some
are sad. A few are quite funny. Several are, frankly, quite terrifying.

The Bible tells us what God says. That's why it's called God's Word.
God's Word comes to us by way of certain human beings. These people
are God's messengers or ambassadors. They are *sent*. They represent
the sender and speak on his behalf. And when they speak, *God* may be
said to speak. So Moses is sent to the Israelite slaves in Egypt. "Go and
say to them," says God. That's often the twin command to messengers.
"Go and say to them, 'I see your trouble and I will save you.'"

Questions about God

The Israelites came to know God through his Word. In this case Moses brought it, and he brought it right into the middle of Israel's trouble.

That's so often where God speaks. In trouble. God's Word addresses us when we are trapped in one way or another. So God speaks liberation to slaves, including people enslaved by their own appetites. The Word of God is meant to lead people out of bondage and into the glorious freedom of the children of God. Once people have their freedom, the Bible gives them some gracious rules, such as the Ten Commandments, that keep free people from sliding back into their trap.

People sometimes get confused about all this. They talk as if the Bible is intended mainly to give us information about God. Not so. The main thing God wants to do with his Word is not to satisfy our curiosity about his nature, but rather to point the way out of our predicament.

We might say that God wants to make us wise — not just wise in general but "wise for salvation."

> O Lord our God, send your Word past our defenses and into our hearts and homes. Rescue us from all that displeases you and drags us down. Through your Word, let us know you as our deliverer. For Jesus' sake, Amen.

How Do We Come to Know God?

3

*And the Word became flesh and lived among us, and we
have seen his glory, the glory of a father's only son, full
of grace and truth. No one has ever seen God. It is God
the only Son, who is close to the Father's heart, who has
made him known.*

JOHN 1:14, 18

The Prologue to the Fourth Gospel has a grandeur all its own. The
verses seem to sing, and with such majesty that even when we aren't
quite sure what they're saying, we still want to hear them. We want to
hear the music in these verses and the eloquence that rolls out from
them. And we want to hear again of a fact so primal, so central, that
the account of it seems to thunder at our door.

"The Word became flesh and lived among us, and we have beheld
his glory."

Words don't come alive for us till they have some flesh and blood
on them. A Civil War officer said he hadn't understood compassion
till he saw Lincoln's face as he sat by a dying soldier. The same goes for
the glory of God. How will we understand God's glory if it stays in
heaven? That's how it goes with words such as *grace* and *truth*. We

don't really understand what God is saying till the Word of God comes to us in a human being.

So the Word became flesh. The Word of God with a name and address! The Word of God with a thumbprint and a building trade! Paradoxes abound now, but, one way or another, all of them show us glory.

Now the feet of God take him to the hovel of a leper, and the hands of God reach to a body that is otherwise untouchable. Now the knees of God bend in front of disciples so that God can wash the feet of men who hadn't dreamed of doing the same for each other. Now the face of God sets itself like flint to go to Jerusalem, the city of death. And the arms of God open to accept a Roman torture and to embrace the world God came to save. Now the voice of God speaks peace to faithful women who have showed up at the tomb on Easter morning to do what was left to do.

In the beginning was the Word, and the Word was with God, and the Word was God. . . ."

That's the way it was from the beginning. But the Word became flesh and lived among us. So now we know something about light and life and love. Now we have a face to put on grace and truth. No one has ever seen God. But we have known God's Son. And that means we have known something of God, because the family resemblance is remarkable.

O God, you have surprised us with your Son. Glory to you, O God. Amen.

How Do We Come to Know God?

4

O Lord, our Lord, how majestic is your name in all the earth! You have set your glory above the heavens. From the lips of children and infants you have ordained praise.

PSALM 8:1-2 (NIV)

In one of his sermons Douglas Nelson recalls the preface to Whittaker Chambers' book *Witness*. Chambers was a convinced Communist and an embittered atheist. But one day he watched his baby as she thoughtfully drooled over the tray of her high chair. He found himself staring with fascination at his daughter's tiny, intricate ear. It seemed to him a marvel. Only a *planner* could have planned that ear. In a conversation that began at breakfast, the cunning shape of his daughter's ear set Chambers on the road to belief.

Believers are often overtaken by creative signs of God. A crocus in March, the angle of an autumn sun on a field, the pattern traced by a desolate bird in flight — these things, and so many others, speak to a believer of God. An infant at her mother's breast, said Calvin, has a tongue "so eloquent to preach God's glory that there is no need of other orators."

We know God, or come to know God better, through creation.

Questions about God

But also through God's providence. A child is rescued; a loved one recovers; a marriage is fastened for good. So many gifts whisper God's name to an alert soul. Music can do it powerfully. So can a nourishing friendship. Even the smell of slow, savory cooking can remind a Christian how good it is to have someone to thank.

Of course, God's providence must sometimes hold us when we are in trouble. Someone's child perishes; a loved one does not recover; a marriage comes unglued. Christians have to come to terms with suffering.

Even then, many believers sense God's care. A lost hiker shivers miserably through a cold night; yet he has never been surer that God is with him. Sad and thoughtful parents visit the scene of their children's airplane crash years after it happened. They are startled by a sudden shaft of sunlight that reminds them that God holds their children. Elizabeth Gray Vining writes of a time when grief had frozen her heart and locked every door in her against any hope. One morning she woke, dull and leaden as usual, to hear what sounded like rain on the porch roof beneath her window. When she got one eye open enough to look, she saw sun streaming in. The patter was not rain but the soft fall of locust blossoms — so many of them that the roof was white! Then and there the ice in her soul began to break up.

> *O LORD, our Lord, how majestic is your name in all the*
> *earth! You whose work is chanted by infants and whose*
> *glory transcends the heavens: O LORD, our Lord, how*
> *majestic is your name in all the earth! Amen.*
>
> — FROM PSALM 8

How Do We Come to Know God?

5

When we cry, "Abba! Father!" it is the Spirit himself
bearing witness with our spirit that we are children of
God.

ROMANS 8:15-16 (RSV)

It's remarkably hard to answer the question, "Why do you believe in God?" So many answers don't seem quite final. You might say, "I believe because my parents taught me." But that's not a final answer. Even wise parents are wrong about some things. They might have been wrong about God.

You might say, instead, "I believe in God because of the Bible and what it says about God." But, again, what if the Bible isn't right? After all, other books disagree with it.

Perhaps you could say, "I believe because God has sent Jesus to save us." But, once more, that answer seems unsatisfactory because you learned about Jesus from the Bible — and the Bible has been set aside for the moment.

Well, then, suppose you say, "I believe because I can see evidence of design in the world." That won't quite clinch the matter either. Perhaps the universe was designed by a beginning team of designers. They were pretty good. For example, they outfitted many creatures with an ingenious blood pump called a heart. But they didn't perfect it. So some creatures have heart failure.

When it comes right down to it, we are hard put to say how we know God. Yet we do. With all our heart we come to know God and his wonderful plan to put things right in a world gone wrong.

How do we know? Perhaps the plainest thing to say, first, is that we have a strong inner conviction. We are *convinced* of God. And we discover that the Bible knows about this strange, unshakable conviction. The Bible calls it the witness of the Holy Spirit.

As it turns out, the Spirit is the hidden persuader in all of our otherwise doubtful sources. It is the Spirit who stimulates childlike faith in what our parents say and do about God. The Spirit witnesses to the truth of the Scriptures, telling us in our hearts that they are from God. The Spirit sparks faith in Jesus Christ, the Son of God. It is even the Holy Spirit who broods over our deep places when we ache with the sense of God in nature.

When in some moment of recognition we call God's name, when after years of prayerless life we begin again, "when we cry, 'Abba, Father!' it is the Spirit himself bearing witness with our spirit that we are children of God."

You, O God, are the one we seek. Behind our masks, we are your children. So let us know your presence and grace, through Jesus Christ our Lord. Amen.

How Do We Come to Know God?

Question 2

What Is God Like?

At the same time we come to know God, we also come to know something about what God is like. Of course, we can't comprehend the one whose greatness overwhelms us. And we are not allowed to sit around and casually "discuss God." God is, after all, unimaginably holy. In any case, God calls human beings more to obedience than to discussion. Yet, because God has graciously disclosed himself, we may reverently ask: Who is God? What is God like?

6

Ephraim is joined to idols — let him alone. Yet it was I who taught Ephraim to walk, I took them up in my arms.

HOSEA 4:17; 11:3

Many couples choose not to have children. It isn't that they dislike children particularly. They just don't want any in their homes and lives. Children need time and take pains. You have to risk and spend yourself for children. You can get attached to children, and they can break your heart.

God has chosen to have children. In Hosea, God's child is called Ephraim, and Ephraim represents Israel and all God's children. God loves Ephraim, but Ephraim has gradually been breaking God's heart. A stubborn prodigal son, Ephraim has been wasting his father's gifts, blackening the family name, and smearing over his own soul with an ugliness that years can't erase.

Along the way, God has given numerous parental warnings. "Don't do that, Son! Look at how you have come to live! You're way off the road. You're in deep weeds and only I can get you out. Come home, Ephraim!"

But Ephraim will not listen. At times it seems he cannot listen.

Questions about God

Finally God lets Ephraim go. He doesn't get even; he just gets out. Here is the ageless picture of a hurt, angry, and deeply disappointed parent. He has said everything there is to say. He has tried everything he can think of. None of it has worked. Now it's time for silence and restraint. "Ephraim is joined to idols — let him alone."

As someone once put it, here is God "pacing the room, biting his lip, hands gripped tightly behind his back." God lets us go, lets us hit bottom, lets us see what life is like in the darkness. If we want to destroy ourselves — well, all right.

And yet, God can't do it. He can't let us go. Isn't God the one who lifted and held us when we toddled into trouble? Isn't he the one who bent to feed our hunger with child-sized bits of food? Hasn't God sat with us many times through the watches of the night?

"How can I give you up, O Ephraim! How can I hand you over, O Israel! . . . I will not execute my fierce anger. . . . For I am God and no mortal" (Hos. 11:8-9).

"For I am God and no mortal." In those words lies the only hope for children who would otherwise make themselves orphans.

> *O God, in you is every grace that restores us. You are the one willing to suffer so that we may be healed. You are the one willing to stoop so that we may stand. Surely you are a God of amazing grace. Through Jesus Christ our Lord, Amen.*

7

To whom then will you liken God, or what likeness compare with him? Have you not known? Have you not heard? The Lord is the everlasting God, the Creator of the ends of the earth. He does not faint or grow weary; his understanding is unsearchable.

ISAIAH 40:18, 28

As we were reminded in the last meditation, God is our Father. For many people that's a sobering thought. Some of our fathers are, after all, not very godly. A number of them are not even very fatherly. God is like *them?* God is like that friendly, confused man at the end of the table? God is like the man who terrorized me when I was young? God is male?

No. But we have to say something about God, even if we know all of our thinking falls short. God is unimaginably greater than we can think. In fact, J. B. Phillips once traced the cause of meager faith to our shriveled ideas of God. *Your God Is Too Small,* said Phillips. Your notion of God is thin and cramped.

So it is. Sometimes it's also absurd. We think of God as a smothering parent or an aging grandfather in his skychair. We picture him as a harassed stock-exchange buyer, trying to handle all the incoming prayers. Or we may find God a blight, a drag on our fun and games, an old-fashioned person trying to hold us back. Our ideas of God are pinched and little. Some are almost blasphemously so. We forget that God is incomprehensibly *great.*

The biblical writers did not forget it. They knew that the Lord is great and greatly to be praised, and that his greatness is unsearchable. They knew, in J. B. Phillips's words, that God is a being of both "terrifying vastness and of minute attention to microscopic detail." God numbers both the galaxies and the hairs of our heads. He is equally concerned with a falling star, a falling sparrow — and a fallen sinner.

"To whom then will you liken God? Have you not known? Have you not heard? The LORD is the everlasting God, the Creator of the ends of the earth."

The remarkable thing is that this great God is also our Father. It's not that he is *either* great or our Father. He is both. The psalmists speak of God's cosmic greatness one moment and the next moment marvel at his patience with a person's single sin and private shame. God and Father. Both.

> *There is none like you among the gods, O Lord, nor are there any works like yours. For you are great and do wondrous things; you alone are God. I give thanks to you, O Lord my God, with my whole heart, and I will glorify your name forever. For great is your steadfast love toward me. Amen.*
>
> — FROM PSALM 86

What Is God Like?

8

Then Jacob woke from his sleep and said, "Surely the
LORD is in this place — and I did not know it!" And he
was afraid, and said, "How awesome is this place!"

An American preacher recalls in one of his sermons that long before
the stories of Abraham, Isaac, and Jacob were written down, Israelite
parents told them to their children. They would tell about Abraham
and Sarah at Gerar — how Abraham once tried to save his own skin by
passing Sarah off as his sister. Sarah never forgot. There was always a
certain look in her eye after that. Parents told stories of blind old Isaac
with his senile cackle, of a blustery Esau, always waving his big, hairy
fists around. Then there were the Jacob stories. Everybody liked those
stories. What a character! What an agile wheeler-dealer Jacob was!

But one particular Jacob story always seemed to catch people by
the heart. It's the story of Jacob at Bethel. In this story, Jacob awakens
from a dream and feels a *presence.* And he is afraid, not because this
presence hurts him, but because it haunts him. Jacob has an awesome
sense of someone from beyond, someone utterly alive and yet wholly
inhuman — someone wholly *other.* Jacob finds himself in the presence of an unspeakable God.

Questions about God

It's a great tragedy that, in an age of instant friends and popular democracy, many Christians are losing the sense of God's holiness. We pray against television background noise. We come into a sanctuary and yak and grin and clap our friends on the back. Our sense of God's holiness has become so weak that we are able to speak familiarly of "the Lord" while stretching our limbs and chewing our gum.

Jacob cannot worship the Lord until he has known the fear of the Lord. He has a hard night on his stone pillow, a night full of dreams and whisperings and old memories. It's an unholy night until Jacob begins to dream. For this shifty, tainted man, it may have been the turning point. It's not that Jacob is able to climb up and lay hold on God. Not at all. He never could. Jacob's God is far above Jacob's ladder. Yet, by this dream and by this ladder, the Holy One of Israel descends to reach for one of his children.

Then Jacob woke from his sleep and said, "Surely the LORD is in this place — and I did not know it!" And he was afraid and said, "How awesome is this place!"

> *Lord God, you are holy beyond our thinking and present beyond all knowing. Even in darkness your light gleams and even in our confusion your truth shines. Surely you are with us even when we do not know it. Through Jesus Christ our Lord, Amen.*

What Is God Like?

9

*He is the image of the invisible God. For in him all the
fullness of God was pleased to dwell.*

COLOSSIANS 1:15, 19

Whoever has seen me has seen the Father.

JOHN 14:9

Douglas Nelson used to tell a story that has been told by Scottish
Presbyterians for years. Somewhere back in the early eighteen hundreds a young boy in Scotland went with crowds from all the nearby
villages to see a hanging. Two laboring men had quarreled with a third
man and had then followed him across a pasture and slipped a knife
between his ribs. After some time the two killers were caught, tried,
and condemned to be hanged.

On a lovely May morning the troops paraded to the very place
where the murder had been committed. There the gallows stood —
black crossbeam and two empty nooses. The criminals were led up the
steps, and the grisly preparations were made. Then the infantrymen
presented arms, the cavalrymen drew their swords, and the drummers
lifted their sticks to start the rogues' tattoo. For just that instant, com-

Questions about God

plete silence reigned across the field and through the crowd. And then, in that hush, a startled lark suddenly soared up from the foot of the gallows. Straight up it shot, as larks do, and the cascading joy of its singing seemed to come from nowhere but heaven. The young Scottish boy later said he could never forget that picture — the pure burst of loveliness in the May sky and, down below, two men kicking and twisting at the end of a rope.

We have seen that same mixture of glory and death before. The disciples who see in Jesus Christ the image of God also see him humiliated and beaten by thugs. They see the face of God's glory puffy and running with other men's spit. They see God's Son groaning over his bloody work. At last they see him dead.

"Whoever has seen me has seen the Father," said Jesus. In their astonishment and pain, the disciples at the foot of the cross must have wondered about that. Only later, only after the first Easter, were they ready to see that God makes life by this death, strength from this weakness, "peace by the blood of his cross."

The "fullness of God" is full enough to take in this suffering and turn it to glory.

What wondrous love is this, O God, that comes with light into our darkness and with the Son of heaven into our hell. Humble thanks to you, O God, for the Christ in whom we see you and know you and come to peace with you. Amen.

What Is God Like?

10

*The grace of the Lord Jesus Christ, the love of God, and
the communion of the Holy Spirit be with all of you.*

2 CORINTHIANS 13:13

24

What is God like? God is fatherly and motherly, as Isaiah 42:14 and
other passages tell us. God is great and holy. God is like Jesus Christ,
his Son. God is, finally and everlastingly, triune.

For centuries before Christ's birth, God's people daily separated
themselves from their neighbors who believed in many gods. The Jews
solemnly reminded themselves that their God brooks no rivals: "Hear,
O Israel: The LORD our God is one LORD" (Deut. 6:4). But with Christ
has come a new understanding of God's oneness. Christians have
come by divine revelation to believe in the holy Trinity.

To this day, Jews believe that Christians have therefore slipped
into polytheism. The Jewish novelist Chaim Potok speaks for many
Jews when he says, "The concept of Jesus as man-God is incomprehensible to the Jewish mind. That concept is pagan. . . . The Jesus
whom Christians talk about — the Jesus who is worshiped — is the
Jesus Jews don't understand."

Here is the root of the doctrine and the problem of the Trinity.
Many Jews don't understand a Jesus who is worshiped. But some Jews

Questions about God

did. That is the way the Christian faith began. Following Jesus' own words and deeds, a small circle of Jewish disciples came to see that this person was to be called Son of God, that he was divine, and that he was to be worshiped. It is Paul the Jew — born under the law, circumcised on the eighth day, trained in the traditions of the Jewish fathers — who calls Jesus Christ "the image of the invisible God." The people who first confessed Jesus as the Christ and the Son of God were sons and daughters of Abraham and Sarah. Salvation is from the Jews. Our Lord was himself Jewish.

So some Jews *did* understand the God-man. From them we have come to know that there is one God — *and* one Lord Jesus Christ. He too is to be worshiped and adored. And this Christ himself speaks of sending the Spirit of Truth — yet another divine person. Thus, for centuries, Christian have worshiped, learned, lived, and hoped in the name of God the Father, Son, and Holy Spirit.

What is God like? The one God is a holy and interlocking Trinity of persons.

> *Triune God, your mystery stretches beyond anything we can feel or think. Show yourself more and more in the mystery of the church, which, though many persons, is one in Jesus Christ. Amen.*

What Is God Like?

Question 3

If the Lord Is with Us, Why Do We Suffer?

A Christian philosopher once addressed an overflow crowd at an Ivy League university. He spoke about whether it makes sense to believe in God. After the speech, a young student stood up and demanded to know how anyone could believe in God after Auschwitz. "How can a good and powerful God allow such horrors? There is no God!"

We Christians believe there is. We have come with all our heart to know God and what God is like. But, as honestly as possible, we have to face the first question asked by those who have suffered or been impressed by suffering: Why? To tell the truth, it's sometimes the first question believers themselves ask: If the Lord is with us, why then has all this happened to us?

11

The angel of the LORD appeared to [Gideon] and said
to him, "The LORD is with you, you mighty warrior."
Gideon answered him, "But sir, if the LORD is with us,
why then has all this happened to us?"

JUDGES 6:12-13

An expert on death and dying reports an incident many of us will understand. A woman came out of a sickroom where a loved one was dying and asked in a tightly controlled voice, "Is there a room anywhere in the hospital where I can go to scream?" A doctor directed her to a place and later mused over the idea that every hospital — maybe every office and home — ought to have a screaming room.

The human voice that calls to God out of suffering often rises to a scream. C. S. Lewis lost his wife to cancer. Just after she died, he wrote down some of the torture of his thoughts:

> Not that I am . . . in much danger of ceasing to believe in God. The real danger is of coming to believe such dreadful things about Him. The conclusion I dread is not "So there's no God after all," but "So this is what God is really like. Deceive yourself no longer."
>
> *(A Grief Observed)*

Questions about God

Lewis mentions the times he and his wife had prayed for a cure. What they got was wrong diagnoses, false hopes, strange remissions, and even one astonishing recovery. But it was only temporary, and the God who held Joy Davidman Lewis in his hands did fearful things with those hands:

> Step by step we were led up the garden path. Time after time, when He seemed most gracious, He was preparing the next torture. . . . I wrote that last night. It was a yell rather than a thought.

A yell rather than a thought. We don't think clearly when we are in pain. We scream.

And it's not unbelief that shouts its hurt or bewilderment at God, but belief. Unbelievers shout their fury at the blind, dumb workings of fate. But believers have to speak somehow with a faithful God who seems at times so absent, so willing to tolerate horror, so far from helping. Generation after generation, believers turn toward heaven to shout their one great question: *Why?*

"My God, why are you so far from helping me?"

"If the LORD is with us, why then has all this happened to us?"

"My God, my God, why have you forsaken me?"

> *O my God, I cry by day, but you do not answer; and by night, but find no rest. Do not be far from me, for trouble is near and there is no one to help. Amen.*
>
> — FROM PSALM 22

If the Lord Is with Us, Why Do We Suffer?

12

*Why is light given to one in misery, and life to the bitter
in soul, who long for death, but it does not come . . . ?*

JOB 3:20-21

Our suffering questions are *why* questions. Why did God permit
Adam and Eve to sin if he knew what evil would come from it? Why
does God allow this, or this much, pain? Why here and now? Why
does God permit children to suffer? And why do the righteous suffer?
Why did Beethoven lose his hearing while rock fans manage to keep
theirs? Why is this gentle person sick and that careless clod healthy?

Some believers, like Job's friends, think they have answers to such
questions. God is testing you, they say. God is punishing you for
cheating. God is fattening unbelievers for slaughter. God foresaw that
if your child had lived longer, she would have left the faith.

The truth is we seldom know any of these things. We may know a
little. We may know why a person has a hangover. We may know how a
person gets venereal disease. We may know why a man who lies can't
get anybody to trust him.

But even here there are surprises. Some liars become presidents.
Some rakes stay healthy. Some drunks rise and shine.

The most truthful answer to our *why* questions about suffering is

Questions about God

that we do not know. We commit ourselves to a God who loves and cares, and by his grace the commitment stays fastened though the mountains shake and the earth moves. We know that in all things God works for good.

But let's face two facts. One is that this good is often hard to find. We can't see it or tell it. God has reasons for allowing *this* crushing humiliation or *that* demonic target-practice, but we do not know what the reasons are. It often seems that we are given a little courage rather than much knowledge.

But let's also face another fact. On the day he died, our Lord shouted, "My God, my God, why have you forsaken me?" Two days later he appeared to his disciples and said, "Peace be with you."

> *O Lord our God, we see in a mirror darkly. But we see there the face of your Son, who suffered for us. Though faith fails and hearts sink, we know that he has led the way through suffering to a peace that passes understanding. In his name, Amen.*

If the Lord Is with Us, Why Do We Suffer?

13

We are children of God, and if children, then heirs, heirs of God and joint heirs with Christ — if, in fact, we suffer with him so that we may also be glorified with him.

ROMANS 8:16-17

People sometimes suffer because of their own sin and folly. Perhaps more often they suffer from the sin or folly of others.

In fact, the New Testament tells followers of Jesus to expect suffering at the hands of others "because of the Gospel" or "for the sake of Christ." Disciples are not greater than their master. Anyone who tells the truth or practices mercy among the unmerciful will sooner or later be opposed. If we do right, we may suffer for it. It's therefore sobering to think of "Christ, our example," and especially in the context of 1 Peter 2:21: "For to this you have been called, because Christ also suffered for you, leaving you an example, that you should follow in his steps."

A few Christians have followed in his steps with the sort of strength that leaves the rest of us in the dust. Douglas Nelson tells of Father Damien, the saintly missionary to the leper colony on the island of Molokai. Damien was much loved by the festering people who had been sent there to get on with their dying. But one Sunday a whole new world reached out and took them in. It happened when, for the first time, Father Damien opened his sermon with the words, "We lepers." For now, under his robes, was a body dying with their disease. And now, in his words, these people heard the voice of Christ.

How shallow we look by comparison! We don't want suffering; we want success. We identify with winners! We don't like lepers or losers very well; we prefer climbers and comers. For Christians, the temptation to be conformed to this world is desperately sweet and strong.

Yet, says the apostle Paul, we are children of God *if* we suffer with Christ. No doubt few of us can follow where Father Damien walked. God does not give his hardest assignments to his weakest children. But a life with no suffering, no embarrassment, no inconvenience for the sake of Christ is not a Christian life.

What, then, must we do?

Lord God, we have sought comfort in things that perish.
Heal us, we pray, for the sake of Jesus Christ our Lord.
Amen.

If the Lord Is with Us, Why Do We Suffer?

14

34

Suffering produces endurance, and endurance produces character, and character produces hope, and hope does not disappoint us, because God's love has been poured into our hearts through the Holy Spirit that has been given to us.

ROMANS 5:3-5

The most general biblical answer to the question of suffering is that we do not know why God permits it. Yet we do know that Christians must suffer for the sake of the Gospel. Father Damien knew it too. The Bible also says that we may suffer from the terrible love of God. Like Jacob, all of us have to wrestle with God. And, like Jacob, we may come out limping. In the severe mercy of God we are wrestled into shape. We may not enjoy the process. But there is no doubt that we are in for it, one way or another.

Kathryn Lindskoog once wrote about these things.

My little nephew John was born with a defective heart. This summer he was six and went to Mercy Hospital for surgery.

A few days later in his oxygen tent, with tubes here and there, the incision still healing, and a nagging thirst . . . John looked at his

Questions about God

mother ruefully with large brown eyes and said simply, "Mommy, I felt better *before* the operation!"

I think John said it for us all. We were all born with defective hearts.

(Eternity)

Conversion is a change of heart. And in some ways we feel better before the operation. The cure is often slow and nearly always painful. We have to whittle down our pride. We have to apologize to people we don't like. We must abandon certain luxuries and then fight off self-pity. We have to do our work the right way even if there is less praise for it that way.

None of us likes this sort of thing. Yet without it we are lost. Old Protestant confessions call the negative part of conversion *mortification*. It means "dying off," and it's no fun. Yet we are going to be put right if it kills us. God works from a model as he molds his children. God has in mind a certain image of how we ought to look. And, as C. S. Lewis says, God pays us the "intolerable compliment" of reworking us until we fit the image.

We know who the model is. We know who is the image of the invisible God. And we know that even this Lord Jesus Christ *learned* obedience through suffering. Even he had to die before he could rise.

O God, we are only pupils of Christ who have to trace his pattern. If there is pain in the tracing, let there also be glory. Amen.

If the Lord Is with Us, Why Do We Suffer?

15

We know that in all things God works for the good of those who love him, who have been called according to his purpose.

ROMANS 8:28 (NIV)

Believers seek not to explain but to live with the presence of evil. They try to do it without losing their faith. Just as children have to trust their parents' judgment that a dental repair will in the long run do them good, so children of God have to trust the strange expressions of God's love.

Sometimes we think we can see what God is doing, especially as we look back at our lives. In a particular defeat God was breaking an addiction. Through a particular pain God was helping us to weep with those who weep. In a world terrorized by hijackers God may right now be outfitting us with courage. No doubt God sometimes lets us suffer vicariously, as Christ did, not so much for our own good as for the good of others. Could it be that saints are sometimes called to bear a fearful disease with grace so as to encourage those of us who are weak? A saint is "a person who makes it easier to believe in God." Perhaps a few words of quiet faith from the lips of a Father Damien can do more good than all the clichés of some thoughtless comforter.

Questions about God

But let's be honest. God's good is often hard for us to understand. In fact, it's sometimes hard to *measure*. As Ernest Campbell remarks, nobody comes on network news to report on the day's gains and losses in goodness. Nobody says, "Forgiveness was up two points today. Courage was off a half. Faith stayed the same." Nobody does that. We have to spot goodness with the eyes of faith, and sometimes we strain to see it.

But it is there, and sometimes in strange places. Douglas Nelson tells of visiting a terrible little cell in the dungeon of an old English castle. No light had ever come there from outside. On one wall the stone had been worn into the shape of a hand, because men dying of thirst leaned there while they licked the filthy moisture that leaked from the moat through one small crack. In that blackness someone had scratched — with a belt buckle, perhaps — the old words of Jacob: "The LORD was in this place and I knew it not."

Even here. Even in this. The Lord is with us for good.

In me there is darkness, but with thee there is light. I am lonely, but thou leavest me not. I am restless, but with thee there is peace. Amen.

— A PRAYER OF DIETRICH BONHOEFFER

If the Lord Is with Us, Why Do We Suffer?

Question 4

How Does God Act?

A number of ancient and modern philosophers believe God is unemployed. They think God doesn't do anything. They believe God is not an actor in the world, but only a factor. God is distant, removed, turned in on himself, shut out of our world by the inexorable laws of nature.

The Bible makes straight such crooked lines of thought. From beginning to end the Bible speaks of a God who acts, who acts in history, and in our history. So we naturally want to know: How does God act?

16

Not one [sparrow] will fall to the ground apart from your Father. And even the hairs of your head are all counted. So do not be afraid.

Children are sometimes afraid. Adults are too. But children's fears are different from adults' fears. Children are afraid of large, friendly dogs who can knock a small person over with a hairy paw. Children fear thunder and blood and "ghosties and goblins and things that go 'bump' in the night." Most children are afraid of the dark, of dark closets, and of those dark places "where the wild things are." When children are lost, they are not merely annoyed. They may be terrified. When children live among irresponsible people, they may think they'll be abandoned.

Jesus speaks to all God's children about a Father's providence. And he speaks to our fear. He speaks to our childlike awareness that in so many ways the world is a fearful place. In such a place the Father knows, loves, and cares for his children.

A theologian who wished to speak of the acts of God might begin with creation. But a child begins with providence. In families that know God, children first learn that God keeps and provides. Children come to know with a wonderful, childlike certainty that even when they are lost or afraid, they are not alone. So in many homes children lay themselves down to sleep, entrusting their very souls to the God who keeps them in the dark and through the night.

God acts in providence. Even a child knows that. But soon children know something else. Soon they know that people sometimes interfere with God's providence in wicked ways. Take food, for example. God gives daily bread for his creatures. Every harvest time God gives food — and skillful farmers to gather and market it. But, strangely enough, the food seldom reaches those who are hungriest for it. Some people keep huge stores of food for themselves, often throwing much of it away. Other people have to get along with very little.

God acts and God provides. But he typically uses us to do it. We needn't fear that God will forget to provide. What we ought to fear is that some profiteer is going to get in the way.

> *God our Father, do take care of all our physical needs so that we come to know that you are the only source of everything good, and that neither our work and worry nor your gifts can do us any good without your blessing. And help us to work faithfully so that we may share with those in need. Through Jesus Christ our Lord, Amen.*
>
> — FROM THE HEIDELBERG CATECHISM,
> ANSWERS 125, 111

How Does God Act?

17

In the beginning . . . God created the heavens and the earth.

GENESIS 1:1

For it was you who formed my inward parts; you knit me together in my mother's womb.

PSALM 139:13

Children ask "why?" nearly as often as philosophy students do. A curious four-year-old can drive us to a confession of the doctrine of creation with about four "whys":

"Why is our car green?"
"That's the color they painted it at the factory."
"Why?"
"Some people ordered green cars."
"Why?"
"Green is their favorite color."
"But why?"
"That's the way God made those people."
"Oh."

Questions about God

It's good to be able to say, "That's the way God made those people" instead of, "I don't know." God has acted in creation, and many of our "why?" questions about our world find their answers somewhere in God's creative plan.

But why did God choose to create at all? Why didn't the Father, Son, and Holy Spirit enjoy their trinitarian fellowship without taking on the task of creating and the burden of caring for an outside world? And why in the world did God find room for the likes of you and me?

Creation is a fruit of God's love. The Father, Son, and Holy Spirit lacked nothing, and yet they freely chose to make powers and persons outside themselves. God creates because he is a loving, fellowshiping God.

At certain times we become especially aware of the greatness of God's creation. On Christmas Eve, 1968, Apollo 8 was returning from history's first flight around the moon. The pictures and accounts of earth as seen from the heavens powerfully moved many who saw and heard them. At the close of one particular telecast, Commander Frank Borman announced that he and the other astronauts had a message for us. With the stupendous view of the revolving earth before him, Borman began to read the first verses of Genesis: "In the beginning, God created the heavens and the earth." The other astronauts took up the reading, and Borman finally finished where God did: "And God saw everything that he had made, and behold, it was very good."

God still creates. For some wonderful reason God has chosen to create you and me. It means that from the beginning we belong to God.

You are the one, O God, who has dug out the depths of lakes, built in the strength of hills, spread out the expanse of the heavens. The whole earth is full of your glory. Amen.

How Does God Act?

18

Now Jesus did many other signs in the presence of his disciples, which are not written in this book. But these are written so that you may come to believe that Jesus is the Messiah, the Son of God, and that through believing you may have life in his name.

JOHN 20:30-31

God's acts in creation and providence are regular enough that we can find natural patterns in them. When we describe these acts with generalizations, we call the generalizations "laws of nature." And laws of nature are good things to have. They let us make plans, do science, stay sane. We note that the planets stay in their orbits. Cannonballs, and even feathers, fall *down* when we drop them. If you go out to the airport and run down a vacant runway, flapping your arms, you will not take off. You don't have nearly enough wingspan. And you can't expect God to make an exception just because you're late for your meeting.

But sometimes God, or God's agent, does do something unusual. Sometimes an action can't be explained according to the laws of nature. When God does an extraordinary act for an extraordinary purpose, we call it a miracle.

Questions about God

Miracles are closely connected with God's other acts. The Bible seldom makes sharp distinctions between God's providence and God's "special" providence. In fact, as Gregory the Great, C. S. Lewis, and others have pointed out, many of Jesus' miracles are small, fast examples of the big, slow acts that God performs all the time. Every harvest God feeds the multitudes with many loaves multiplied from a few grains. Every summer, along sunny hills, God turns water into wine. Jesus does the same thing fast and on a small scale. He just does what he sees his Father doing. There is, as Lewis put it, a kind of "family style."

But God's family never does miracles just for the fun of it. Miracles are not mere magic. God's Son doesn't care to dazzle people who want to gape. No, miracles are "signs." Miracles attest to the power of God and the presence of God's Son. Miracles tell us in miniature and in brief what is always true on a grander scale. They say "God at Work!"

What follows is that miracles are serious things. The point of a miracle is to save people. Think of the Exodus. Think of the Resurrection. Think of the fact that Jesus did many other signs so that we may believe and "have life in his name."

> O Lord our God, we know you are not only good but also great. We know you are able to do strange and wonderful things. Let us not be so skeptical that we fail to see them. But neither let us be so greedy for signs that we fail to see the slow, steady wonders of creation and providence all around us. In Jesus' name, Amen.

How Does God Act?

19

But when he came to himself he said, . . . "I will get up and go to my father, and I will say to him, 'Father, I have sinned.'"

LUKE 15:17-18

46

A recent writer recalls the story G. K. Chesterton tells about a boy who left his home on an English mountainside. The boy was searching for a remarkable thing he had heard about since babyhood. It seems that somewhere, outlined on distant hills, was the shape of a giant man. It was a kind of miracle, people said, how the giant had taken shape in the hills. The boy decided he must see that shape. He must discover that giant if it took all his life. Across the valley he trudged, hoping to see the miracle on the next row of hills. It was not there. But, as he turned to get his bearings, he looked back. And there, where he had come from, the white limestone rocks formed the outline of a giant. In its heart was the house he had left. He had been too close to the giant to see it.

The greatest act of God's providence happens close to home. It happens so close to home we may not see it. God's great miracle is to breathe new life into our own collapsed lives. Theologians call it regeneration. Jesus calls it being born again.

Questions about God

Adam and Eve left the Garden. The Prodigal Son left home. We have all tried somehow to break out of the embrace of God to seek our happiness in a far country. We have been told of wonders and pleasure there.

But not all the reports are true. Life in the far country is futile. Its days are empty and its nights cold. Only when we turn and look back do we discover what we had been seeking, and that's the place we've left. The trouble is that it takes pains — something like birth pains — to get out of the far country and back home to the real world.

Unless we are born anew, said Jesus, we cannot even *see* the kingdom of God. No doubt the Prodigal Son began to see it for the first time when he said, "I will get up and go to my father, and I will say to him, 'Father, I have sinned.'"

47

> *What wondrous love is this, Lord God, that seeks us when we are runaways from home and draws us back to live and feast with all your other children! Through Jesus Christ our Lord, Amen.*

How Does God Act?

20

But, in accordance with his promise, we wait for new heavens and a new earth, where righteousness is at home.

2 PETER 3:13

48

Redbook magazine once printed the story of Janet Zorick, whose husband died in a terrible fire in a crowded building. She too had been in the fire, but her husband had lifted her over his head and had thrown her forward toward the exit. Though she was badly burned, Janet Zorick escaped. Her husband did not.

For months afterward Janet couldn't sleep. She remembered in ghastly detail the sight of people on fire, of husbands who "just kept going when their wives were knocked down," of her own husband's look of horror as he picked her up. She remembers his gasping, "One of us has to get out for the kids." She recalls how she felt when his blackened watch was returned to her and what an indignity it seemed to her that he was found with only one shoe on.

Later, Janet Zorick tried to sort through some of the agony of her thoughts. Though she and her husband were both strong, church-going Lutherans, she had, for a time, great difficulty believing in God. How could he have allowed such a tragedy?

Questions about God

Finally, though badly shaken, her faith came back. Again and again she concluded that she *had* to believe in God — and in the life to come. God had reached for her husband in a horrifying way, but it must have been God into whose presence her husband was received. Otherwise, she concluded, nothing means anything. "There has to be a hereafter or what's the use of anything?"

At the borders and crises of life, Christians have always looked for anchorage to the great biblical truth that our little careers are not the whole story. To conclude his great work of creation, providence, and redemption, God will finally bring history to a climax and usher in a new heaven and a new earth. This is the last and most splendid act of the drama. Part of its glory is that all God's children will be gathered for feasting and rejoicing.

Christians do not let this vision hinder their concern for the present world. They do let this vision give them confidence. In fact, there are times, as for Janet Zorick, when the vision of heaven seems our only hope.

> *O Lord, you are the light of the world, ever shining, never going down. Draw us, and all creation, to the final dawning of your light. Amen.*

How Does God Act?

Question 5

Why Pray?

A Christian graduate student invited his professor home for dinner. As was his family's custom, the student offered a prayer before the meal. Afterward, the professor said, "You might as well have whistled."

Was the professor right? Is prayer a kind of whistling in the dark? Does anyone hear us when we pray? Is anyone listening? Christians wish to speak with God. Can we? Does it do any good?

Why pray?

21

So if you have been raised with Christ . . . be thankful.

COLOSSIANS 3:1, 15

In one of his books, John Baillie tells of a time he attended a religious service conducted by a humanist. The service included a sort of prayer of thanksgiving, in which the humanist avoided saying, "We thank you, O God," and substituted the words, "We are thankful."

It must be an odd feeling to be thankful to nobody in particular. Christians in public institutions often see this odd thing happening on Thanksgiving Day. Everyone in the institution seems to be thankful "in general." It's very strange. It's a little like being married in general.

Christians are thankful to God, and especially because they have been raised with Christ. Prayer is the most important way of saying so. Thanksgiving is the healthy, upbeat response from people who know God's goodness.

Take just one dimension of a good life: God has arranged things so that we human beings link to each other in a wonderful web of dependencies. So we give thanks for people who fight fires, dam floods, set bones, teach children, treat depression, play music, make kites, refurbish ghetto houses, plant trees, and struggle to get a widow's case to

Questions about God

court before her witnesses go stale. Especially we remember those who do these things in the name of Jesus Christ.

And most especially we give thanks for the Savior himself — the one for whom we are named, the one who blesses us and rescues us even when we have turned our backs to him. As Graham Greene's priest says in *The Power and the Glory,* Jesus Christ came to save not only pimps and thieves, but also half-hearted Christians. Who can be thankful enough for the Savior of indifferent people?

God gives and we give back. Thanksgiving is the natural response for those who have been raised with Christ to join the family of God.

> *God of Life, who has loved us into life, your shepherding care guides and sustains us. You have nourished us with bread of fields, bread of friendship, bread of Providence, and the living Bread of Christ. How can we thank you as we ought? We would be thankful in prayer and deed and inmost spirit; through Jesus Christ our Lord. Amen.*
>
> — FROM THE BOOK OF COMMON PRAYER

Why Pray?

22

If we confess our sins, he who is faithful and just will forgive us our sins and cleanse us from all unrighteousness.

1 JOHN 1:9

Nobody wants to confess sin. It scuffs our pride. It doesn't sound like possibility thinking. So we skip it. Or we print out the short list instead of a full account. Or we mumble ("I'd just like to share that we're going to be targeting holiness as a growth area today").

The problem is that sin is like garbage. You don't want to let it build up. Confessing sin is like taking out the garbage. You want to do it regularly because taking out the garbage is an extremely healthy thing to do.

After giving thanks Christians confess their sins. They confess the sins everybody knows, and the ones God only knows. They confess to God not just because it's so good to have a garbage-free soul, but especially because our sins grieve God, and we want to say we're sorry. We're sorry we have ignored God for weeks at a time. We're sorry we've been leading a double life. So much to be sorry for. We've tied our feelings of self-worth to success on the job rather than to God's grace. We've spent more money in one week for fun and games than we spend in a whole year for feeding the poor.

What does a person actually do in confession? She says, "I did it, and it was very wrong." "I should have done it, and I never did." "O God, I have been far away from you, and I want to come back." "O Lord, forgive me, cleanse me, heal me." "O God, I did not make myself, cannot keep myself, can never forgive myself. Please save me."

Robert Roberts has written that Christian confession of sin happens "inside the cradle of grace." The One we have grieved by our sin can be grieved just because he loves us. And the one who loves also saves. In confession we look for mercy, assurance, and the profound consolation of knowing how far God is willing to go to redeem us.

Create in me a clean heart, O God, and put a new and right spirit within me. Do not cast me away from your presence, and do not take your holy spirit from me. Restore to me the joy of your salvation, and sustain in me a willing spirit. Amen.
— FROM PSALM 51

Why Pray?

23

The might of your awesome deeds shall be proclaimed,
and I will declare your greatness. They shall celebrate
the fame of your abundant goodness, and shall sing
aloud of your righteousness.

PSALM 145:6-7

Some people are never satisfied. They think others drive too slow and eat too fast. They're convinced government is crooked, the schools are worthless, and the church is full of hypocrites. Something is wrong with every sermon these people hear, every program they see, every dish of food they are willing to try. Such people seem to spend the whole of their sour little lives in front of a complaint window. They are like the pessimistic farmer who had six chickens hatch one morning. He was inconsolable. When someone asked him what was wrong, he replied bitterly: "I had six chickens hatch this morning, and now all of 'em have died on me but five."

Open, grateful human life resounds not with complaints but with praise. The healthiest people are the ones who praise the most. Family, friends, books, sports, music, nature — all these things draw praise from healthy people: "Did you see *that?* Wasn't it great!" "Did you hear what she did for her sister? Isn't she a generous person!" C. S. Lewis once described praise as "inner health made audible."

Christians reserve their highest praise for the goodness and greatness of God. The psalms ring with it: "The LORD is great and greatly to be praised! Praise the LORD!" At creation, says the Book of Job, "the morning stars sang together, and all the children of God shouted for joy."

Praise is a way of expressing awe and admiration for the almighty love, the all-loving might, of God and for the ingenious ways in which God keeps fitting his help to our need. Our prayers ought to include some hearty praise. But whether in prayer or other speech, praise of God is still a form of prayer, and calls to do it may never be glib. "Praise the Lord" is not just another way to say "Have a nice day!"

God of Grace and God of Glory, you are great and greatly to be praised. You are kind and deeply to be loved. We adore you, before whom angels hide their faces. You are Life and Light. You are journey and home. We bow before you, asking nothing, save that our life may be your flame. Glory be to you, O Lord most high! Through Jesus Christ our Lord, Amen.

—— FROM THE BOOK OF COMMON PRAYER

Why Pray?

24

Then Jesus said, "Father, forgive them; for they do not know what they are doing."

LUKE 23:34

58

Then [Stephen] knelt down and cried out in a loud voice, "Lord, do not hold this sin against them." When he had said this, he died.

ACTS 7:60

Some people teach children to pray for others by looking at their hands. The thumb, which is closest to their hearts, reminds them to pray for those who are nearest — for family, loved ones, and neighbors. The index finger, used to point, expresses authority and reminds them to pray for teachers, police, and parents. The middle finger, the highest one, reminds them to pray for presidents, prime ministers, and "all who are in *high* authority." (In some cultures, the middle finger reminds Christians to pray for enemies, and in some cultures enemies and people in high authority are one and the same.) The ring finger is the weakest, as all pianists know; it reminds children to pray for those who are poor, betrayed, sick, marginalized. Finally, the little finger reminds them to pray for themselves, that God may have his way in their lives. They come last.

Questions about God

Four out of five prayers make requests for others. We call such prayers *intercessions*. In intercession we play the part of priests, going into God's presence for the sake of another. Intercessions are especially fragrant and loving prayers.

The bright pattern of intercession runs through the Bible. Moses pleads for the children of Israel; Paul for his young churches; our Lord, and Stephen after him, for enemies. Here, as someone has said, is prayer in a major key. Here is prayer that is twice blessed. When God hears and answers such prayer, God blesses those for whom we pray. But simply by praying such prayers, we too are blessed. Why? Because it's almost impossible to remain self-absorbed or angry when we humbly pray for the good of others.

But does our neighbors' good actually depend on our prayers? Well, why not? After all, in God's world our neighbors' good often depends on our work. Perhaps, at least some of the time, the same is true of our intercessions.

So let us pray.

> *God of the common good, who has bound us in one bundle of life, we plead our neighbor's need. For the nations we pray: give peace in our time. For the workers of the world we pray: gird them and us that none may lack bread, since you have given enough for all. For the sorrowing and the sick we pray: make their shadow the secret way of your coming. For our friends and loved ones: befriend them in your own befriending. Remember in your mercy those whom we forget. Gather all needy folk within the healing of your wings. Teach us to bear one another's burdens, that we may fulfill the law of Christ; for his sake. Amen.*

— FROM THE BOOK OF COMMON PRAYER

Why Pray?

25

Ask, and it will be given you; search, and you will find;
knock, and the door will be opened for you.

MATTHEW 7:7

A petition is a solemn request. Even children know about petitions. Sometimes they are passed around at school. Children are asked to sign the petition; then they wait to see what happens. Adults know about petitions too. Someone passes around a petition, we sign it, and then the matter is never heard of again.

That's not quite true. Sometimes those whom we petition *do* act. But not always.

Faithful people have always brought petitions to God. We ask God to do things. Jesus taught his followers to ask. When we ask God for things, we show dependence, expectation, maybe even residual thankfulness. But sometimes believers ask God to do something wrong: "Rise up and humiliate my enemy, O Lord." Sometimes believers ask God to do what he can't do without rejecting someone *else's* petition: "Let our side win, O God." Occasionally, believers ask God to give strange gifts: "Let me have the power to become invisible, O Lord, and I will become a thorn in the side of organized crime."

But most often believers ask God for seemingly innocent — even

Questions about God

necessary — things. They ask that a disease be healed, a marriage restored, a daughter protected. Sometimes God grants these requests, but sometimes not. And we wonder why. At times our wonder turns into bafflement and fury.

"Ask, and it will be given you." But do I have to stand here every night, yelling like a fool into the darkness?

"Search, and you will find." But do I have to search twenty years for some hint that my son believes in God?

"Knock, and the door will be opened to you." I *am* knocking. I have been knocking until the door is splintered and my knuckles are raw. And no one answers.

What must we say to this? On the one hand, we have such strong, ringing assurances from the lips of our Lord. But, on the other hand, here we are with our strained voices, dashed hopes, and bloody knuckles.

How do these things go together?

> *Our Father in heaven, hallowed be your name. Your kingdom come. Your will be done, on earth as it is in heaven. Give us this day our daily bread. And forgive us our debts, as we also have forgiven our debtors. And do not bring us into the time of trial, but rescue us from the evil one. For the kingdom and the power and the glory are yours forever. Amen.*
>
> — FROM MATTHEW 6

What Has God
Called Us to Do?

We have seen that God acts and that believers respond in prayer.
But there is more. We have to do something besides praying. We
have to go to work. We have to follow a vocation. Is a vocation
only a job?
    What has God called us to do?

26

We are what he has made us, created in Christ Jesus for good works, which God prepared beforehand to be our way of life.

EPHESIANS 2:10

Sometime after he resigned from office, Richard Nixon revealed that the worst of his personal tortures was a loss of vocational purpose. He observed that in Southern California a number of people seem to live purposeless lives. They gather at expensive watering holes, where they eat too much, drink too much, talk too much, and think too little. They lack goals. They lack any sense of lasting achievement. These people are overfed but undernourished. Sooner or later they show the strain.

One of our deepest hungers is for purpose. God intends that hunger to be fed by our vocation.

Most ideas of a vocation are much too narrow. People who have stumbled aimlessly into tending bar, advertising electric card shufflers, or administering a state lottery may tell of their "vocation," but you get the impression they are only describing their job.

The biblical writers talk another way. In the Bible, vocation is a vast and broad idea. It means God's calling. First, God calls unbelievers to repent and believe the Gospel. When they do, they get a second vocation. The second call, strange to say, is to enlist in the military! The church — the church militant — is God's army for fighting the remaining evil in the world. All Christians are called to take part:

> Enemy-occupied territory — that is what this world is. Christianity is the story of how the rightful king has landed, you might say landed in disguise, and is calling us all to take part in a great campaign of sabotage.
>
> (C. S. Lewis, *Mere Christianity*)

The campaign is on. What has God called us to do? We are to pray. That is the chief part of our thanksgiving for the King's landing. The other part is *doing good* for the kingdom. In this we at once find our vocation and our life's purpose. Into this life's vocation of doing good for Christ's sake each of us must fit his or her work, play, and relationships. "Your kingdom come," Jesus taught us to pray. And then he gave us the translation: "Your will be done on earth as it is in heaven."

> *Dear Lord, help us to direct all our living — what we think, say, and do — so that your name will never be blasphemed because of us, but always honored and praised. In Jesus' name, Amen.*
>
> — FROM THE HEIDELBERG CATECHISM,
> ANSWER 122

What Has God Called Us to Do?

27

*"Strive first for the kingdom of God and his righteous-
ness, and all these things will be given to you as well."*

MATTHEW 6:33

Jesus witnessed to the kingdom of God, and Jesus' resurrection vindi-
cated his witness. In Jesus Christ, God's kingly reign showed through
much more clearly for a time. Jesus' exorcisms demonstrated God's
authority over demons that stir in us. Jesus' healings showed God's
power over diseases that sicken us. Jesus' nature miracles — walking
on water, making lots of wine for a wedding celebration — previewed
the wonders of God in the age to come.

We now live between Jesus' first and second advents. During his
first coming, Jesus brought God's kingdom near (Mark 1:15), but Jesus
also pointed toward the fullness of the kingdom still to come. In his
earthly career Jesus changed the world, but he didn't perfect it. He
healed many sick people, but not everybody. He cast out some demons, but not all. So far as we know, he turned water into wine only at
Cana. He invited just one disciple to walk on water, and with mixed
results.

So in his first advent Jesus did much, but he also left much to do.
Remarkably, he left much for his followers to do. He told them to ask,

Questions about God

seek, and knock; to "strive first for the kingdom of God and his righteousness." He asked them to "let your light shine before others, so that they may see your good works and give glory to your Father in heaven." At the end Jesus told his followers, then and now, to "make disciples of all nations, baptizing them and teaching them to obey everything that I have commanded you" (Matt. 7:7, 33; 5:16; 28:19). In short, Jesus called all of his followers, including any of us today who believe in him, to participate in the kingdom as its agents, witnesses, and models.

Salvation is a gift of sheer grace, which God intends to flow through saved persons and out to others. The kingdom of God is the place where the flowing is to happen. Christians who go with the flow are simply following their vocation.

67

Give us, O Lord, open minds to seek your will, soft hearts to receive your will, and ready hands to do your will. Through Jesus Christ our Lord, Amen.

28

Let each of you look not to your own interests, but to the interests of others.

PHILIPPIANS 2:4

Bear one another's burdens, and in this way you will fulfill the law of Christ.

GALATIANS 6:2

If our main calling is to strive first for the kingdom of God, we might also have a number of sub-callings, including our occupations. God's kingdom includes many of these. A person could be called to be a machinist, a homemaker, or a zookeeper. Some people are called into the ministry. God calls some of us to live for him as persons with disabilities in nursing homes. Many Christians do so with the kind of grace that arises from a platform of great courage.

The possibilities are nearly infinite, and extend beyond my occupation. So how do I know God's will for my life?

Some people expect God's call to come as a flash in the dark or a voice in the night. After all, the Bible records such calls. Such people might expect to graduate from college, come home, and have a helpful

Questions about God

family friend look them squarely in the eye and say, "Forest Management!" So off they go into forest management.

But often God's call comes less dramatically. You size up your training and experience. You get a sense of your gifts and interests. You face your limitations. (Thus, you may *know* God has not called you to be a concert flutist.) Meanwhile, you inform yourself of current needs. Flight controllers, for example, are more in demand than stagecoach builders. And through it all you pray as honestly as you can. You ask God for wisdom.

You do something else. Recognizing the communal dimension of all Christian vocation, you consult with other Christians. None of us needs to make a vocational decision alone. Others may know of gaps Christians need to fill. We ought to cultivate a sense of each other's gifts — possibly, in some cases, even of each other's *duties.* Other Christians can see in us things we haven't spotted. In the Christian community, we may expect to hear things like this: "Ralph, your heart isn't in this work. Have you considered a change?" "Barbara, you have strong gifts in this area. Why not work toward a degree?" "Jim, your children are over-mothered and under-fathered. I wonder if you need to stay home more."

Other Christians may speak what we later regard as the summons of God himself. Those who find themselves obeying such a summons have the opportunity to live a life instead of merely making a living.

Search me, O God, and know my heart; test me and know my thoughts. See if there is any wicked way in me, and lead me in the way everlasting. Amen.

— FROM PSALM 139

What Has God Called Us to Do?

29

Do not be conformed to this world, but be transformed
by the renewing of your minds, so that you may discern
what is the will of God — what is good and acceptable
and perfect.

ROMANS 12:2

In one of his books, Richard Mouw takes up a vocational problem that vexes many Christians: the problem of vocational *witnessing*. On the job, or in my broader calling, how do I bear witness to what God has done and is doing?

Consider a businesspersons' prayer breakfast. A group of lively Christians gets together in the morning to pray, eat breakfast, and urge each other on to witness on the job through that day. They discuss contacts, strategy, witnessing failures, and successes. They ask each other: "How can I use my business contacts today to tell someone what Jesus has done for me?"

These are devout brothers and sisters in Christ. Unfortunately the prevailing idea at their breakfast is that each of them is a businessperson who *also* wants to witness about Christ. The Christian faith is seen as something *extra*; it adds something to the job, but it doesn't get worked deep into the bones and innards of the job itself.

Questions about God

Consider a harder, but more excellent, way. A group of lively Christians gets together to pray, eat breakfast, and discuss strategy for demonstrating the lordship of Christ *in* their business practices that day. They ask: "How, today, can we write a policy, sell a house, lobby for a law, advertise a product, in a way that honors Christ and makes God's name more respected? How can we do justice, love mercy, and walk humbly with God as members of our profession? How can we keep our jobs and still do what is right? How can we avoid being conformed to this world and yet work effectively in it as transformers of culture for Christ's sake?"

Of course, these Christians may also be required to give verbal witness to Christ. But, if so, the witness will not be tacked on to their job; it will not be something extra. No, the witness will tell why these Christians do their jobs the way they do and who inspires them to do it.

God has called us to discern his will, to make it our own, and then to exhibit it by doing good in the world. Worldly people snicker about "do-gooders." Christians do not. Christians know that every day presents good opportunities to "strive first for the kingdom."

> *We want to be weavers, O God. Teach us to weave together our work and witness into a seamless garment that warms others and that shows forth your beauty in the world. Through Jesus Christ our Lord, Amen.*

What Has God Called Us to Do?

30

We know that our old self was crucified with him so that the body of sin might be destroyed, and we might no longer be enslaved to sin. So you also must consider yourselves dead to sin and alive to God in Christ Jesus.

ROMANS 6:6, 11

Suppose I join with other Christians in doing the work of the Lord — as a homemaker, as a computer salesperson, as a deacon, as a shut-in, as a volunteer firefighter, as a congresswoman. What sort of life will fill my months and years? What may I *expect* in my vocation?

Two things: dying and rising. All Christians are called to this dying-and-rising pattern we inherit from our Lord himself.

Veteran Christians know something about on-the-job mortification. They know that doing a job right means taking pains. A devout housing contractor builds up to code even when his competitors do not — and can therefore underbid him. A worker patiently puts up with a neurotic boss. A whistle-blower is fired for his forthrightness. A businesswoman loses an account because she will not lie to her client to get it. In fact, every Christian who rejects vocational shortcuts and chiseling will suffer and die a little.

But Christians also experience a vocational coming-to-life. All of us want to be happy. Our happiness is directly tied to our feelings of self-worth. But the old trap is always set: do well in your vocation and you are worthwhile; fail and you are worthless. It's the devil's attack on the grace of God.

So the coming-to-life of the new self depends on faith. Christians trust God with a faith that *keeps us from measuring our self-worth by how well we are doing* — on the job, at our hobbies, in our homes, as parents. Of course we should do as well as we can. But we should do it in freedom, in the confidence that we are deeply treasured by God even when we have blundered into some outstanding failure!

Christians are called to take delight in every bit of good God gives us to do. We are to enjoy a big Christian freedom that lets us fail with regret, but also with a sense of humor, and that lets us succeed with joy, but also with quiet humility.

Gracious God, in all our living help us to be genuinely sorry for sin, to hate it more and more, and to run away from it. Then give us wholehearted joy and delight in doing every kind of good you give us the chance to do. Through Jesus Christ our Lord, Amen.

— PARAPHRASED FROM THE
HEIDELBERG CATECHISM,
ANSWERS 89, 90

What Has God Called Us to Do?

Questions about Humanity

Question 7

What Are We Like as Fallen?

Perhaps John Calvin's most famous observation is that our knowledge of God is unbreakably linked to our knowledge of ourselves. After focusing for thirty meditations on our knowledge of God, we turn to look at ourselves and to ask some questions about humanity.

A theologian might ask at once about our origin as good creatures of God. But our experience of ourselves has to start where we do — as creatures entangled in sin. So we begin by asking, What are we like as fallen human beings? Of course we have to deal here with a secular society and culture that is saturated with all the sin and sadness that have come down to us from the Fall. But we know the question deals with us too, with who we are except for the grace of God.

31

Formerly, when you did not know God, you were en-slaved to beings that by nature are not gods.

GALATIANS 4:8

In 1976, Alex Haley published a powerful book that deeply influenced American culture. In this book Haley traces his ancestry from an eighteenth-century African village, through American slavery, to the present. *Roots* is a moving and extraordinary search for human identity. All of us, says Haley, are dependent on ancestral tradition to know who we are.

Well, who are we? For millions of people interested in their roots, the question can become a passion. Who am I? Who or what defines me? How do I most basically identify myself?

Contemporary culture offers many answers. You can take a fair sample of them, as someone has noted, simply by watching the almost weekly parades along New York's Fifth Avenue. Each parade has music and the same politicians wearing determined smiles. Only the banners change. One week they say, "I love St. Patrick!" The next week, "I'm Greek-American." I'm Hispanic or Norwegian or gay.

People define themselves by sex, race, class, religion, ethnic group, family, occupation, education — even by club membership or astrological sign. "I'm a war veteran." "I'm a Mormon." "I'm a seventh-generation descendant of Kunte Kinte." "I'm a sixteenth-generation descendent of a seasick *Mayflower* passenger." "I'm a Vassar woman." "I'm a Hell's Angel." "I'm a Capricorn."

We grope among the roots of what the apostle Paul calls "human tradition" for some way to fill in our ID cards (Col. 2:8). The trouble is that when we pin our ultimate loyalties to these traditions, when we make them our final comfort, we commit the sin of idolatry. "Your god," said Martin Luther, "is whatever your heart clings to."

Post-modern people have wanted to define themselves, and their definitions have gotten complicated: "I'm a union woman of Romanian and African descent." Christians believe that the Word of God defines us. For *all* human beings, the first answer to the question, Who am I? is this: "I'm a fallen creature of God." But only some people trump the first answer with a second. They're the ones who can go on to say: But now I'm a Christian.

> O Lord our God, we can't claim to be pure in our loyalty to you and to your Christ. We are too much the products of our culture and too little the products of your Holy Spirit. We pray for those who still try to define themselves. And we pray for ourselves, that you may have your way with us. Through Jesus Christ our Lord, Amen.

What Are We Like as Fallen?

32

Now the serpent . . . said to the woman, "Did God say,
'You shall not eat from any tree in the garden'? You will
not die; for God knows that when you eat of it your eyes
will be opened, and you will be like God, knowing good
and evil."

GENESIS 3:1, 4-5

At least two generations of young Americans were raised on Horatio Alger novels. Under various titles (*Do and Dare, Sink or Swim, Try and Trust*), Alger wrote the same novel repeatedly. In it a poor but virtuous lad ("our hero") would struggle by luck and pluck to rise from rags to riches. Usually he had a widowed mother. Typically a rich man (perhaps a wicked "Squire") and his snobbish son would try to ruin the widow and humiliate our rising hero. Nearly always the virtuous lad would appear on his first date with a girl whom the snobbish boy also liked — but didn't dare approach. Whenever this happened, the rich boy would accuse our hero of "putting on airs." Then he would rest his case by declaring, "You don't know your *place!*"

"You don't know your place!" There isn't much room for an accusation like that in a popular democracy. For centuries certain people have blocked or oppressed other people to "keep them in their place."

Questions about Humanity

Whites have done this wickedness to blacks, rich to poor, men to women. Victims of such oppression have naturally wanted to be free, and wonderful people have tried to help. Democracy is God's gift.

But a great spiritual danger always accompanies the democratic spirit. The danger is that we may seek to rid our lives of not only human but also divine dominion. The danger is that we human beings will forget who made us and to whom we belong. The danger in a popular democracy is that we may try to democratize God. If we don't like God's program, if "our eyes are opened" and we conclude that God isn't necessarily any better qualified than we are, we can simply vote him out and run for office ourselves.

Without the influence of the Gospel, we are tempted to see ourselves as self-governed. We are forever tempted to answer the question: Who is the lord of your life? with the breathless voice and shining eyes of fools: Is it *I?*

Outside of Christ we do not know our place.

> *Great God, you are the one who puts down the mighty from their thrones and scatters the proud in the imagination of their hearts. We pray for the proud; we pray for ourselves, that you may have your way with us. Through Jesus Christ our Lord, Amen.*

What Are We Like as Fallen?

33

When the crowds saw what Paul had done, they shouted . . . "The gods have come down to us in human form!" But Jews came there . . . and won over the crowds. Then they stoned Paul and dragged him out of the city, supposing that he was dead.

ACTS 14:11, 19

In one of his sermons Wallace Alston tells of the difficulty some young people have in "facing life's incredible demands." He mentions a high school teacher who gave his students the chance to ask him anything they wanted — and to do it anonymously. The students asked, of course, about sex, about drugs, and even about life on other planets. But, says Alston, "Believe it or not, the question most frequently raised was that of *suicide*."

Teenage suicide, which was almost unheard of a couple of generations ago, has now become a problem and a horror great enough to alarm parents and to prompt national television reports. Even some nine-year-old children fall into depressions so deep that they are tempted by life's ultimate lonely act. Since 1997, some of the suicides have come at the end of bloody shootings in America's schools.

Why? Experts talk about a broad sense of hopelessness in young

Questions about Humanity

lives: some young persons are convinced that they and their lives matter to nobody.

The tragedy is that some of them may be right — at least as far as other human beings are concerned. It's a tragic fact that in a secular society we turn some young persons into popular idols and others into throwaways. Sometimes we even do it to the same person.

That's what happened to Paul and Barnabas at Lystra. One moment the people of Lystra kissed the dirt at Paul's feet; the next moment they tried to kill him. First they wanted to worship Paul as a god; then they wanted him dead.

Before we are saved, this same fickle streak colors our view of *ourselves*. One day we may see ourselves as precious, the next day as worthless. Looking at ourselves outside of Christ, we want either to worship or to destroy, either to bow down or to bow out. We see ourselves in an unfocused image that is always shifting between pride and despair.

As fallen people, we do not know our place.

Merciful God, raise up Christ in those who have fallen into the deepest darkness. And with Christ in them, raise up hope. Around hope, please raise up faith and love. We pray for the hopeless. And we pray for ourselves, that you may have your way with us. Through Jesus Christ our Lord, Amen.

34

The man said, "The woman whom you gave to be with
me, she gave me fruit from the tree, and I ate." . . . The
woman said, "The serpent tricked me, and I ate."

GENESIS 3:12-13

At three I had a feeling of
Ambivalence toward my brothers.
And so it follows naturally
I poisoned all my lovers.
But now I'm happy; I have learned
The lesson this has taught;
That everything I do that's wrong
Is someone else's fault.

In this folk song, Anna Russell jabs at the no-fault ethics of certain
psychiatrists, who have developed an allergy to personal guilt. The allergy has spread. People accused of graft in public office defend themselves by pointing to a tradition of graft in that office. Divorce is rou-
tinely seen as a kind of happening that everybody is powerless to
prevent. The same goes for adultery. These things "happen."

Deep in our fallenness is the urge to shrug off personal blame. We

Questions about Humanity

see it early on in the lineup of figures in the Garden — each pointing a finger at someone else. And we keep on seeing it in the familiar attempt to fix blame on heredity or environment:

"I can't help it if I have a rotten temper! It runs in my mother's family."

"It's not my fault I can't hold a job! My second-grade teacher called my safety-first poster rubbish. That cut me down as an artist. If she hadn't done that, I might have become another Andrew Wyeth."

Apart from the gospel of Christ, we are tempted to say we have no sin. We are tempted to see ourselves not as sinners but as *victims*, not as fallen but as frustrated, not as wrong but as misunderstood or underestimated.

We deceive ourselves, and the truth is not in us.

Lord God, without a sense of your holiness, we can't see our sin. Let us know your holiness, and then let us know our sin. We pray for the shameless; we pray for ourselves, that you may have your way with us. Through Jesus Christ our Lord, Amen.

What Are We Like as Fallen?

35

Cain said to the LORD, "My punishment is greater than I can bear! . . . I shall be a fugitive and a wanderer on the earth, and anyone who meets me may kill me."

GENESIS 4:13-14

The story of Cain and Abel is one we've heard before. It's a crime story so old and deep in the history of the human race that it's gotten the status of a legend — a *true* legend. In this story the crime is murder and the motive is envy. What's striking is that Cain kills his brother, but then he can't get the murder to be over. He can't get the dead man to stay dead! Abel's blood keeps crying out from the ground. In fact, it cries to high heaven where God hears it. Cain kills his brother Abel, and the sound of the killing goes on and on. Frederick Buechner says it's the astonished bleating sound that an innocent man makes on the day his brother sticks him with a pitchfork.

What's striking in the story is not only Cain's terrible violence, but also his childlike pathos. Cain is a man who discovers that he needs the same God he had opposed. He hadn't wanted to obey God ("Am I my brother's keeper?"), but neither does he want to lose God. And so when God banishes him, Cain first protests ("My punishment is greater than I can bear!") and then grieves ("I shall be hidden from your face!").

Questions about Humanity

Cain doesn't want to go to the land of Nod, because God isn't there. The way to tell is that the land of Nod is full of killers. It's full of fugitives just like Cain. And that makes it a fearful place. Cain knows that if he leaves the land of God and enters the land of Nod, he won't be the only man with a pitchfork.

Outside the arch of God's blessing, we are all fugitives and wanderers. We are displaced persons, lonely for God even when we don't say so, afraid of each other, exiled from home.

And the last place of exile — a place of our own making — is hell.

> *Dear Lord, unless you embrace us, we are unloved. Unless you gather us in, we are scattered on the earth. We pray for those who are still aliens. And we pray for ourselves, that more and more you may have your way with us. Through Jesus Christ our Lord, Amen.*

What Are We Like as Fallen?

Question 8

What Are We Like as Redeemed?

People tend to make two mistakes when they think about the re-deemed life. The first is to underestimate the sin that remains in us; it's still there and it can still hurt us. The second is to under-estimate the strength of God's grace; God is determined to make us new.

As a result, all Christians need to say two things. We admit that we are redeemed sinners. But we also say boldly and joy-ously that we are redeemed sinners.

36

For I know that nothing good dwells within me, that is, in my flesh. I can will what is right, but I cannot do it. For I do not do the good I want, but the evil I do not want is what I do.

ROMANS 7:18-19

Anyone who has ever tried to stick to a diet knows some of the exasperation with which Paul explodes in this chapter. You *know* what's right. It's right to abstain from glazed doughnuts. It's right to become slimmer and trimmer. And yet, as you pass the bakery in your supermarket or as your hostess offers you a chocolate mousse or as you try to slip by the Nut Shoppe just as they are roasting some truly scandalous cashews, you are called into battle once again. Something in you is perversely, outrageously at war with what is right. Something in you wants the evil *you* do not want! And occasionally this enemy succeeds in melting your firmest resolution as a hot apple danish melts a lonesome and defenseless pat of butter.

Later, the guilty deed done, you sit down for an earnest talk with yourself. "Look, self," you say, "you were supposed to be done with all that. Why did you do it again? That's not what you really want!" And so on.

Questions about Humanity

"I can will what is right, but I cannot do it. For I do not do the good I want, but the evil I do not want is what I do."

Fallenness is complete slavery to sin. In that slavery we don't even want what is right. On the other side, the perfection for which God intends his saints means complete and powerful freedom from sin. Perfect people not only want what is right; they invariably do it.

We are, meanwhile, in between. Because of the profound work of Jesus Christ, we are no longer slaves to sin. We are now slaves to God. But we are still learning the ropes, still learning obedience. We are no longer dwellers in the land of great darkness. But we have not yet arrived at the city of God. We are pilgrims. We are on the way.

We all live in the tension of being redeemed but not yet perfected. We know the sin in us has met its Conqueror. But we also know the conquering will not be complete until *for us,* as for himself, our Lord says, "It is finished."

> *O Lord God, loosen the hold on us of everything but your Holy Spirit. We are divided persons; unify our lives. We are double-minded; give us the single mind of Christ. O God, in your grace, break the power of sin over us so that even when we fall back into its embrace, it cannot hold us. In Jesus' name, Amen.*

What Are We Like as Redeemed?

37

You are not your own. . . . You were bought with a price.

1 CORINTHIANS 6:19-20

92   Let's face the truth. We're not always willing to live for God. Even when we're willing, we're not always *ready.*

Still, the idea of serving the kingdom of God does strike sparks in us. Why? We've been made by God, saved by God, forgiven by God. *We belong to God,* and we've taken covenant vows to say so. Besides, the kingdom of God has lots of good employment openings.

And yet, in other chambers of our heart there are beds open for older romances — or maybe for some new love that can brighten the tattletale gray in the midlife of faith. We'd like a god that's a little more responsive to our wishes, maybe one of those portable gods like the golden calf Aaron made for the Israelites. A god of our dreams. A golden god from our past. A god, as Karl Barth says, that lives by our imagination and art, a god from *our* storehouse of riches and memory, a god for the interim, a god for the silence of God, a god for the absence of our mediator. A god that is as good as gold.

Your god, said Martin Luther, is whatever your heart clings to, but that's the problem because our hearts are torn. We are divided people. We love two gods. We love them both. Every day, as C. S. Lewis said:

Questions about Humanity

We try, when we wake, to lay the new day at God's feet; before we have finished brushing our teeth, it becomes *our* day and God's share in it is felt as a tribute which we must pay out of "our own" pocket.

(The Problem of Pain)

Who will deliver us from this body of death? Who will cut off our foreign affairs? Who will finally end our old love-affair with ourselves?

> *O God, we are divided people. We cling to you but also*
> *run from you. We do love you, but we love our own lives*
> *even more. Again, let us die and rise with Christ, and*
> *then again till our old self has drowned at the bottom of*
> *the Red Sea. Amen.*

What Are We Like as Redeemed?

38

God so loved the world that he gave his only Son.

JOHN 3:16

So you also must consider yourselves dead to sin and alive to God in Christ Jesus.

ROMANS 6:11

Evelyn Newman tells a story about a minister who came upon two boys and a dog. In a friendly, patronizing way, the minister asked the boys what they were doing. "Well," said one boy, "we found this dog, and we're going to have a contest for him. Whichever of us can tell the biggest lie gets to keep the dog."

The minister was shocked. "Boys," he said. "That's terrible! Why, when I was your age, I never told any lies!"

There was a moment of silence. Then one boy shrugged and said, "Well, I guess *he* gets the dog."

It's a great mistake to underestimate the sin that clings to a redeemed life. Ministers who act as if they've never said Shucks, evangelists who promise converts non-stop joy, people who say they have no sin — all these deceive themselves. We are redeemed *sinners*. And we need our Savior.

Questions about Humanity

But much more remarkably, we are *redeemed* sinners. And sometimes we've missed the force of our redemption. Old hymns describe us as "worms." Some church forms tell us to "loathe ourselves." Craig Barnes once started a sermon on repentance by remarking that all of us flinch at the topic, because we expect the minister to say something like *"Bad dog! Bad, bad dog!"*

In a lively book written from the center of Western Michigan Calvinism, a culture ripe with guilt and self-accusation, Anthony Hoekema wrote these words:

> Many of us tend to look only at our depravity and not at our renewal. We have been writing our continuing sinfulness in capital letters, and our newness in Christ in small letters. We believe in our depravity so strongly we think we have to practice it, while we hardly dare to believe in our newness.
>
> *(The Christian Looks at Himself)*

We hardly dare to believe in our newness, and the reason is not that we're so humble. The reason is that we're not so faithful. We secretly think Jesus isn't up to the job of saving us. So we consider *others* "dead to sin and alive to God" because we think love requires us to give them the benefit of the doubt. But we won't give ourselves the same benefit.

Would it help to recall an observation of Lewis Smedes? In one of his books, Smedes says that the gospel tells us not only how bad pride is; it says the same about despair. It tells us not only that we needed to be died for; but also that in God's gracious judgment we are *worth* dying for.

You, O God, are the light of the minds that know you, the life of the souls that love you, and the strength of the wills that serve you. Amen.

— A PRAYER OF ST. AUGUSTINE

What Are We Like as Redeemed?

39

Put away your former way of life, your old self, corrupt and deluded by its lusts. Clothe yourselves with the new self, created according to the likeness of God in true righteousness and holiness.

EPHESIANS 4:22, 24

Most of us have a rough idea what an *image* is. Look in a mirror. The thing that grins back foolishly at you is not you, or even your face, but your face's image. You can't touch the image, but you can see it. It's very real.

We see images in other places. We see them in the viewfinders of our cameras. We see them chiseled into marble and painted onto canvas. We see them even in our own minds. If a light is flashed in your eye a certain way, you will "see" an after-image even after the light is off and your eyes are shut.

We also have a small library of mental images of other people. You can call to mind the face of a loved person, even one who has been dead for years. You can picture that face — the shape of the nose, the set of the eyes, the characteristic half-smile.

An image is a kind of counterpart, a duplicate, a likeness. And a

Questions about Humanity

most striking and mysterious thing the Bible says about us is that we are made, and are now being remade, in the *image of God.*

What does that mean? It's hard to say. Theologians have been arguing about it for years. Part of the reason for the argument is that the Bible doesn't give a precise explanation of the image. But it does include goodness, righteousness and holiness, knowledge and dominion (Gen. 1:31; Eph. 4:24; Col. 3:10; Gen. 1:28; Ps. 8:4-8). Perhaps *every* created and recreated perfection is part of the image of God.

One thing follows immediately. The perfections that are part of our "new nature" must be reflected in our *self-image.* Of course daily repentance is a part of daily spiritual hygiene. But the sin we reject belongs more on the border than in the center of our self-image. Aren't we images of God! Doesn't Scripture testify that we're being renewed in knowledge, righteousness, and holiness to conform to Christ! Isn't it a plain fact that almighty God thinks we are people worth dying for!

Did we really think he was only salvaging junk?

O Lord our God, please move us away from the old things, the old self, the old manner of life. Let us put on Christ, including faith, hope, and love. In his name, Amen.

What Are We Like as Redeemed?

40

*Then God said, "Let us make humankind in our image,
according to our likeness." . . . So God created humankind in his image . . . male and female he created them.*

GENESIS 1:26-27

Certain people have "charm" or "presence." As a modern novelist
notes, it's not that such people have been to charm school. They've not
endured all the "Be Likable and Make Friends" courses. (You can tell
the trained charmers by their memorized phrases, slick smiles, and instant chumminess.) No, a genuinely charming person will have her
own dignity and personal reserve. But the center of her interest is outside herself. She has a highly developed awareness of *you*. Her attention stays fastened to what you say. Her focus centers itself on what is
worthy and interesting in you. She has the ability to make you feel special.

All of us are deeply responsive to such treatment. We are
charmed. The reason for our response is that in the attention paid and
received we see a striking image of God.

From the last meditation we might have concluded that the image
of God is some individual quality that each of us must cultivate. But
in fact the image of God shows up especially in our life together. A

Questions about Humanity

wonderful reflection of God's nature is the sort of communion, fellowship, and mutuality that results when we love one another.

Think it over. At the beginning, as now, it wasn't good for the man to be alone. So God designed a fitting partner. Communion was set up on earth as it is in heaven. The very God who loves — who begets a Son and, with the Son, breathes the Holy Spirit — says, "Let us make humankind in our image." From the beginning we were meant to be together.

We have been estranged from each other for a long time now, sometimes fearing the same persons we love. Sin has gotten between us. But now a triune God — a *social* God — is breaking down the dividing walls of hostility and building his church, which is the only authorized model of the holy Trinity in all the Scriptures.

A Prayer of Jesus for the Church:
"As you, Father, are in me and I in you, may they also be in us. . . . The glory that you have given me I have given them, so that they may be one, as we are one" (John 17:21-22).

What Are We Like as Redeemed?

Question 9

How, Then, Should
We See Ourselves?

In the last group of meditations we concluded that the Bible's message about us is positive and hopeful. Though we are still divided persons — tugged at both by the world and God — God's tug is stronger. We are redeemed *sinners.*

As we've seen, the question naturally follows: How, then, should we see ourselves? This is a question of self-image, and a delicate one. Is it an unseemly question? Self-interested all over again? Dangerous?

Let's see.

41

It was in Antioch that the disciples were first called "Christians."

ACTS 11:26

As we have seen, people identify themselves in a host of ways. Some do so proudly: "I'm a Canadian." "I'm rich." "I'm a *mean* hombre!" Some do so in despair: "I'm a failure." "I'm a loser." "My sister is a CEO and I'm a buffoon."

Very often we begin to see ourselves as others see us. We take over their descriptions of us and make them self-descriptions. Thus, a young boy might never think of himself as "poor" until somebody else describes him that way. A teenage girl might never think of herself as "attractive" until some wonderful person makes that pleasant observation. An athlete might never think of himself particularly as an animal until his basketball coach says to him, "Klankenfelder, you are a real *horse* on the boards."

"In Antioch the disciples were for the first time called Christians." For the first time they were nicknamed, and they probably didn't like it very well. They had thought of themselves as disciples, brothers, believers, followers of Jesus. "Christian" — probably said with a sneer — was a nickname chosen by outsiders.

Questions about Humanity

Yet the name has stuck. We have taken it over. We now see ourselves as Christians. We aren't first Hispanic or Asian-American or WASP. Not first men or women, boomers or busters, seniors or 'tweens. Those are all secondary distinctions. We are first Christians. That's what identifies us.

But is it enough? Does the term still tell enough?

Ernest Campbell has observed that in a standard dictionary, when you get down to about the third definition of the word *Christian*, you read things like this: "Christian: a decent human being." In some circles you are Christian if you are kind to Granny and civil to the IRS.

But, of course, being decent is not enough. To be full-blooded Christians, we have to be baptized into Christ's death and resurrection and then spend a lifetime "keeping the rhythm going." To be a Christian is to be a follower of Christ — one who follows Christ down into death and back up into life.

In Antioch or anywhere else, only *disciples* deserve to be called Christians.

O God, we confess to you that we have seen ourselves as others see us; we have seen ourselves as we would like to be. Now, in your grace, change us into the likeness of Christ, and then let us see ourselves as we really are. Amen.

How, Then, Should We See Ourselves?

42

So if anyone is in Christ, there is a new creation: every-thing old has passed away; see, everything has become new!

2 CORINTHIANS 5:17

People who hear sermons and read Christian literature come on a number of phrases that seem more familiar than clear. One of these is the phrase "in Christ," which appears more than 150 times in Paul's letters. Lewis Smedes once wrote a whole book about this little phrase.

Paul says Christians are elect in Christ; they die in him and are raised, sanctified, and blessed in him. They are enriched in Christ, wise in Christ, safe in Christ. The whole church is one body in Christ. Paul himself claims to be bold; to be established; to have power; to speak truth, exhort, labor, rejoice, and hope — all in Christ.

What does any of this mean? How could a twentieth-century person get "in" a person such as Jesus Christ? Does Paul mean that each of us mystically merges with the person of Christ? That we are some-how absorbed into his personality? That we become divine in this way?

Probably not. When Paul talks about being "in Christ," he is first of all speaking historically. The main idea is that by Christ's death and

Questions about Humanity

resurrection — that is, in Christ — God was "reconciling the world to himself" (2 Cor. 5:19). God was renewing an old and partly ruined creation by means of historical events.

To be in Christ is to belong to the people of those events and of all that they mean.

Here's an analogy. At 11:00 p.m. on September 15, at every state government seat throughout Mexico, thousands of Mexicans celebrate their independence with a reenactment of Father Miguel Hidalgo y Costilla's "el Grito de Delores." In 1810, this aged Creole priest ordered the arrest of Spaniards living in Delores, Guanajuato. He then rang the church bell, summoning his parishioners not to Mass, but to revolution. His rallying cry ("el Grito)" started a movement whose end in 1821 meant freedom from Spain, not only for Mexico, but for all of Central America. Today, Mexicans stage this event every year. On September 15, at 11:00 p.m., they shout "Viva Mexico!" and sing their national anthem. Flags unfurl, fireworks flare, and cathedral bells toll.

Maybe only a few Mexicans think of themselves as being "in Hidalgo." But all Christians see themselves as being in Christ. They see themselves as members of the community that owes its very existence to the events of Christ. By ritual acts, by name, by history, by self-image, Christians say: We are the people of Christ's cross and resurrection and of all that they mean.

For our heritage and history, for the communion of saints across the ages and across the world, for life in Christ, we give you thanks, O God. Amen.

How, Then, Should We See Ourselves?

43

You have been cut from what is by nature a wild olive tree and grafted.

ROMANS 11:24

Twenty-first century people have come to know a particular pattern of selfishness. Selfish people do not care for those at the borders of life — for people who are old and about to die or for those who are young and about to live. Self-absorbed people try to pull in their lines, tie off their responsibilities, and hunker down into the pleasures of middle-aged adolescence.

This means trouble for children. In some places abortions out-number live births. Men make babies and then ignore them, hoping their son or daughter will not bother them or require their love. A depressing seventy percent of parents who responded to a columnist's inquiry stated that if they had it to do over again, they would not have had any children. It wasn't worth it.

But some children who escape the machinery of abortionists and the slower death by neglect at the hands of their natural parents are let out for adoption. Many of them are almost immediately placed. Others wait. Some of those who wait are disabled. Some are members of more than one race. Nearly all, as they grow older, become excruciat-

Questions about Humanity

ingly aware that someone rejected them. They keep on waiting for someone to open a door and invite them into their homes and lives.

One of the truly gracious moments in a hard world is that moment when caring parents undertake to adopt such a child. From human brokenness a child has been conceived and born. From that same brokenness the child is now delivered. Of course, an adoption can't by itself solve all problems. Some adopted children struggle for years with the knowledge that their life began with rejection. Many find it appalling that they know nobody to whom they are related by blood. Still, they often enjoy a whole circle of brothers, sisters, or friends. They know they belong again. They belong to parents who are attempting one of the most delicate of all grafts.

Christians are members of Christ and of his community, family members of the household of faith. Perhaps today, with all the warmth God gives us, we can see that we ourselves are his adopted children.

> *O Lord, we are all your adopted children. From our loneliness and fear you have graciously redeemed us. Now let us turn with that same grace to those who are still alone. Through Jesus Christ our Lord, Amen.*

How, Then, Should We See Ourselves?

44

Vindicate me, O LORD, for I have walked in my integrity, and I have trusted in the LORD without wavering. I do not sit with the worthless, nor do I consort with hypocrites; I wash my hands in innocence, and go around your altar, O LORD.

PSALM 26:1, 4, 6

A Princeton preacher retells an old story about a minister who looked out over his congregation one Sunday and asked, "Is there anyone here who has achieved perfection?" No one answered, of course, for if anyone *had* achieved perfection, he or she would have been much too modest to mention it. So the minister tried again, asking if anyone had known, or even heard of, someone who was perfect. Immediately a man got to his feet and shouted, "My wife's first husband!"

We sometimes get the impression that the psalmists are much like this first husband. C. S. Lewis and others have wondered about the degree of self-approval one finds in such biblical places as Psalm 26. Isn't this psalmist too good to be true? Isn't he ready for heaven right now? Parents of small children notice that when they discipline one child, the others reach up to adjust their halos and begin to speak piously: "God doesn't like what Nathan did, *does* he Mommy! I *never* do that,

Questions about Humanity

do I!" Some of this piety sounds a little like a children's version of Psalm 26!

Well, as Lewis says, "We must not be Pharisaical even to the Pharisees." Only the self-righteous say, "I thank you, Lord, that I am not like others. I thank you that I am not self-righteous." But it doesn't follow that *every* attempt to do what is right makes a person self-righteous and that every attempt to do good makes one a contemptible "do-gooder." That's a typical postmodern error — to think that it's better to be a scoundrel than a prude.

But enemies of the Christian faith are right to warn against self-righteousness. It's a terrible danger to a healthy life before God. As soon as we see ourselves as redeemed, we may begin to congratulate ourselves. As soon as we see ourselves being made holy, we may start to see ourselves as holier-than-thou.

Would it help if we reminded ourselves that we are only beggars telling other beggars where to find food?

> *O Lord God, we have set strict standards for others and have made plenty of allowances for ourselves. We have shown more interest in being right than in being kind. Forgive us, O God, through Jesus Christ our Lord, Amen.*

How, Then, Should We See Ourselves?

45

But all of us who are Christians have no veils on our faces, but reflect like mirrors the glory of the Lord.

2 CORINTHIANS 3:18 (PHILLIPS)

You can do some things well only if you aren't watching yourself do them. You can't watch yourself swing if you hope to hit a baseball. You can't watch yourself go to sleep. You can't watch yourself pray. You can't even watch yourself *play.*

Itzhak Perlman, the violinist, was once asked about public playing. "You are the center of attention of four thousand people," said the interviewer. "Some are violinists themselves. In front of all those people you have to do terribly intricate work and do it all from memory. How do you keep from freezing up with fright?"

Perlman's answer was definite: "You can't think about being the center of attention. You can't think about all those people. You can't think about how secure your memory is. You have to lose yourself in the music, or else you'll never play well in public."

One of the traps in our whole line of questioning must now be admitted. We've been asking: How, then, should we see ourselves? We've been asking about the Christian's self-image. We've been looking inside.

Questions about Humanity

But that's good only for a while. Then it has to stop. A violinist will analyze his technique from time to time. But he has to forget all that self-analysis when he actually begins to play music.

So it is with the Christian life. Mature Christians don't get self-conscious. They don't let their right hand know what their left hand is doing. They don't spend their lives in analysis: "Hey! Look at me! How'm I doing?" Healthy people take their temperature when they have a fever. Neurotic people take it every day.

Paul makes the astonishing claim that we are mirrors of the Lord's glory. His glory. Not ours. Our job is to reflect away from ourselves a glory that doesn't belong to us. The idea is to "lose ourselves in the music."

Exodus tells us that Moses was exposed to the glory of God on the mountain. Then the inspired writer tells us that "when Moses came down from Mount Sinai . . . he did not know that the skin of his face shone" (Exod. 34:29).

Lord our God, let us lose ourselves in seeking your will and find ourselves by tracing your pattern for our lives. If by the way you make us shine, O Lord, let us be the last to know. Through Christ we pray, Amen.

How, Then, Should We See Ourselves?

Question 10

World and Christian Community:
How Do We Fit?

Christians are citizens of two cities and inhabitants of two worlds. On the one hand we are human beings and citizens of the city of humankind. But, remarkably, we are also redeemed human beings and citizens of the city of God. We are in the world, but not of the world. We belong to the community of human beings, but, more especially, we belong to the community of God.

What is our relation to each? Where in the world do we fit? And how in the world do we fit into a Christian community?

46

*[Potiphar's wife] caught hold of [Joseph's] garment,
saying, "Lie with me!" But he left his garment in her
hand, and fled and ran outside.*

GENESIS 39:12

It is hard to flee and look dignified at the same time. Slapstick comedians count on this. So do kids. That's why kids love to scare people, especially grown-up people. Grown-ups look funny when they flee. Except, of course, if the danger is real. It's not funny to see someone move quickly away from a rattlesnake. But if you flee from a rubber snake, all the kids in the neighborhood will giggle. The joke's on you.

To a certain sort of secularist, Christians are themselves a joke. Especially Christians who flee from evil. In films and plays, a Christian man who detours around a saloon or backs away from a whore is ridiculous. He's afraid of something harmless! There's the joke.

Well, nobody likes to be a joke. No Christian likes to beat a hasty retreat while people stand around and snicker. That's why Christians sometimes go along with what's wrong. They can't bear ridicule.

With a glint in her eye, Potiphar's wife said to Joseph, "Lie with me." What if Joseph, wishing to keep his options open, had said, "Look, let's have a drink and see if this is something we both can handle?"

Questions about Humanity

But he left his garment in her hand, and fled and ran outside. A ridiculous figure? Charging out of the house minus his bathrobe! What's he *afraid* of?

He's afraid of sinning against God. And he's willing to lose both his garment and his dignity if he can keep faith with God.

God calls us out of the land of Egypt, out of the house of Potiphar's wife, out of the world. Godly people from Abraham to the disciples of Christ are a chosen people, called out of the world to do the good works prepared for them. The calling is continuous. Every day we are re-called.

Thus a Christian in the world is like a Christian at a party that has taken an ugly turn. Sometimes we just need to get up and walk out. We don't belong here.

Will people laugh? Perhaps. They may think the danger is imaginary. But Christians are not so naive. They have a healthy fear of sin. They know the danger is real. And they will flee even if they can't look dignified at the same time.

> *In your mercy, strengthen us, O God, against the power of laughter. Then, in your strength, send us back to those who laugh with a good work and a good word that bring Christ to them. Amen.*

World and Christian Community: How Do We Fit?

47

*God is faithful; by him you were called into the fellow-
ship of his Son, Jesus Christ our Lord.*

1 CORINTHIANS 1:9

116

Certain people are *individualists*. They think the individual is more
important than the group. In religion, they are afraid of the social gospel. In politics, they are more afraid of socialism than of anything else.
They believe that sovereign individuals may band together by a "social
contract" to form a corporation, a state, or even a church, but that in
any case the individual is primary and the group secondary. The
group is there only for the sake of the individual. A French political
scientist once said: "Individualists owe nothing to anyone; they expect
nothing from anyone. They acquire the habit of always considering
themselves as standing alone, and they are apt to imagine that their
whole destiny is in their own hands."

Christianity is against individualism. In the Old Testament God
made his covenant with Abraham and his descendants, with a whole
people. We now baptize persons not because they are individual believers or even because they belong to a family of believers, but because they belong to the extended family of believers — the people
of God. We are all baptized into this community, into a body that

Questions about Humanity

existed long before we did. We do not join this body. We are called into it.

When God's people are called out of the world, they are called into fellowship, into what the New Testament calls *koinonia*. Good words are associated with *koinonia*: "common," "commune," "commonwealth," "community," and "communion." We were called into *koinonia*, which means we have something in common with other believers.

Rather, we have some*one in* common. The New Testament uses many pictures for this reality. We drink from a common cup of blessing; we break a common bread; we are connected as branches to a common vine; we are fingers and toes of a common body. But always it is Jesus Christ who is the fount of blessing, the broken bread, the life-giving vine, the head of the body. We belong to him — and thus to each other.

As a noted Canadian thinker has said, "Only fallen people are individualists."

> *We know, O God, that it is not good for us to be alone. We will never be strong enough, wise enough, or mature enough to keep from stumbling. So give us strong fellowship in the Holy Spirit. Amen.*

World and Christian Community: How Do We Fit?

48

Why should my liberty be subject to the judgment of someone else's conscience?

1 CORINTHIANS 10:29

Certain people are *collectivists*. They think the collective, or the group, is more important than the individual. In religion, they are afraid of individual Christian liberty and distinctive expressions of Christian faith; collectivists believe that everyone must do and believe the same thing. In politics, collectivists are more afraid of right-wing republicanism than of anything else. They believe that the company or the state or the church may wish to grant the individual certain freedoms, but in any case the group is primary and the individual secondary. The individual exists only for the sake of the group.

Some collectivists in the church can't stand to see anyone alone. "Togetherness" is their password and solitude their enemy. They are always trying to organize groups. Even when their groups break up, it's only to break up into smaller groups. In small groups, people share. Some groups hold hands and tell secrets. People are hemmed in, crowded together, pressured into intimacy. They begin to yearn and grope for some breathing room. They recall gratefully that the apostle Paul says something about *individual* Christian liberty.

Questions about Humanity

Christianity is against collectivism. None of us may separate himself or herself from the community. On the other hand, the community must not erase our individual differences, rip away our secrets, or mash us all into the same mold. The "melting pot" image is not found in the Bible.

Each of us needs to respect the liberty and personhood of others. Christians come in many shapes, colors, ages, and sizes. They come in two sexes and from different ethnic origins. They come married and single. They exist at different levels of maturity. For some of us, faith is colored especially by emotion, for others by reason, for others by moral sensitivity. Some of us drink wine; some do not. Some of us are teenagers; some of us have been Christians for seven decades.

Certainly the dividing walls of hostility have been broken down. Certainly we are one in Jesus Christ. But we are not one *glob*. We are one body. And that is a very different thing.

> *Keep us, O Lord God, from trying to make over our brothers and sisters in our own image. Give us a delight in the vast variety of ways and persons by which you reflect your glory. In Jesus' name, Amen.*

World and Christian Community: How Do We Fit?

49

Now you are the body of Christ and individually members of it.

1 CORINTHIANS 12:27

How do we fit into the Christian community? We're not sovereign individuals who contract to get together for convenience. We're not a blob of Christian togetherness. We are "the body of Christ and individually members of it."

In one of his matchless speeches, C. S. Lewis reminds us how specially Paul meant this term "member." When we talk about the members of a political party, for instance, the word "member" means something very different from Paul's use of the same word. Members of a political party are nearly indistinguishable. Each is simply a voter, or worse, "a vote." One person, one vote.

But members of the body of Christ are at once very dependent on each other and very different from each other. They are like bodily organs or parts, as different from each other as an eye is from a hand — and just as coordinated. Our unity is a "unity of unlikes," an organic unity, a complementary unity. And the body of Christ moves into action only when each member is doing his or her part.

This idea is first a disturbance to us and then a source of great security. It is first a disturbance because it puts us at odds with our culture. Our culture exalts either the individual or the group. It exalts individual preferences, individual rights, individual morality, even individual religion. On the other hand, it also exalts politically correct group-think. In group-think, you are free to express your own ideas, just so they're the same as everybody else's. Since we Christians reject both individualism and collectivism, we constantly rub against our culture.

But membership in the body of Christ is also a source of great security for us. It allows us to be ourselves, to do what we can do, to play our role in the communal drama. We enjoy both the satisfaction of group fellowship and the liberty of personal differences.

What could be better? We are "the body of Christ, and individually members of it."

O Lord God, we pray for the body of Christ, for the church and all her members. Let us work together while at the same time we rejoice in our diversity. Let us care for those members who are weak. Let us build your kingdom, through Jesus Christ our Lord. Amen.

World and Christian Community: How Do We Fit?

50

Come to me, all you who are weary and are carrying heavy burdens, and I will give you rest. Take my yoke upon you, and learn from me; for I am gentle and humble in heart, and you will find rest for your souls.

MATTHEW 11:28-29

This is rest; give rest to the weary.

ISAIAH 28:12

On a frosty night in *David Copperfield* Davy goes to bed, "a little bed which there was just enough room to get into." He describes a feeling of security in the nest that makes even adults wriggle more deeply into their chairs:

> . . . when the door was shut and all was made snug (the nights being cold and misty now), it seemed to me the most delicious retreat that the imagination of man could conceive. To hear the wind getting up out at sea, to know that the fog was creeping over the desolate bar outside, and to look at the fire . . . was like enchantment.

Questions about Humanity

Is that a picture of the Christian community? A "delicious retreat" from the world? An ark to ride out the storm? A private snuggery where we can pull the covers over our heads while the heathen rage outside? Does God offer us that kind of blanket protection against the cold? When Jesus said he would send a Comforter, did he mean a kind of quilt?

No. God is our refuge as well as our strength, but never for hiding away. In the rhythm of dealing with us, God calls us out of the world to strengthen us and send us back.

So there is no staying in bed until "the storm of life be past." We have to be ready to step out onto the cold floor, pull on some clothes, and go out into the night. Someone's hunger needs food. Someone's courage needs shoring up. Somebody is finally ready to hear a word from the Lord.

"Come to me, all you who are weary and are carrying heavy burdens, and I will give you rest." It's a beautiful invitation and rightly loved. But let's not forget that the same Christ who calls also warns us to count the cost. The same shepherd who loves his sheep also sends them out among the wolves. The same Lord to whom we go for rest fits us with his yoke to go out and bear the burdens that would otherwise break our hearts.

We come to you, O Lord, with our burdens to lay down.
And you offer us a cross to take up. What an odd kind
of rest you give! But what a relief to know that we bear
burdens in yoke with you. Amen.

World and Christian Community: How Do We Fit?

Question 11

Male and Female:
How Are We Related?

We move now to our last question about humanity. It's a sensitive one, closely related to who we are, how we see ourselves, and how we fit in the world and the Christian community. How are we related as males and females?

Several of these meditations have been influenced by Lewis Smedes's Sex for Christians, *a book I heartily recommend.*

51

*And the man and his wife were both naked, and were
not ashamed. Then the eyes of both were opened, and
they knew that they were naked.*

GENESIS 2:25; 3:7

Everybody knows that people are interested in sex. Ministers know
that if they preach about sex, people's attention will not wander and
their eyes will no longer glaze over. Booksellers know that many people are in the market for maps of their erogenous zones and diagrams
of the way of a man with a woman. Advertisers know that sex will sell
not only high fashion wear, but also light trucks and shampoo.

Meanwhile, for several decades Christians have been asking about
traditional gender roles and attitudes. Should men always take the
lead? Is an aggressive woman more remarkable than an aggressive
man? There are many differences between male and female today. Did
God intend all of them? Or did we invent some? What *is* the main difference?

It's hard to miss the physical difference. God made it. For Adam
God made a match, a fitting partner, a human person like Adam himself — but with the fascinating difference. For a time that difference
between male and female or (Hebrew) *'ish* and *'ishshah* was inno-

cently enjoyed in all its ripe, sensual fullness. God had knowingly designed his human beings to come together, cling together, *cleave* together. They were not ashamed of their difference. As Vernard Eller once put it, there was nothing between them — nothing to fear, nothing to hide, nothing to cover up. They had decent exposure.

But then it happened. In the Fall the man and woman lost their innocence, and they knew it. On perfect human beings nakedness had looked good. But with sin came shame and cover-up. With sin and shame came a distortion of male and female relations that still causes misery all over the world. Persons of both sexes find themselves with sexual disorders they did not choose. Regions of the world get known for the "sex industry" there. In myriad ways, men dominate women, and women let them do it. The domination humiliates women, and in some parts of the world it kills them — places, for example, where women lack the cultural clout to say No to diseased men who insist on having sex with them.

Sexism isn't just bad manners. It's not just that men call women "broads" and expect them to take it. Sexism is a humiliating and sometimes lethal corruption of a match made in heaven.

Sexism is a prime reason the world needs a Savior.

O Lord our God, we confess to you the sin that has so long spoiled our relations together as male and female. We have been not only awkward but also arrogant, not only shy but also deceitful. We have been deeply confused. Save us, O God, through your Word and Spirit. Amen.

Male and Female: How Are We Related?

52

There is no longer Jew or Greek, there is no longer slave
or free, there is no longer male and female; for all of you
are one in Christ Jesus.

GALATIANS 3:28

Arthur Schopenhauer, the nineteenth-century German philosopher, wrote an essay "On Women" in which he said: "As nurses and educators of our children, women are suited precisely in that they are themselves childish, simple, and shortsighted; in a word, grown-up children, a kind of middle step between the child and the man — who is the true human being."

Sad to say, statements only a little less sexist may be found among ancient Christian writers and theologians. According to some of them, women are weak, slow-witted, and unstable. They're a "necessary evil," a "domestic peril," and the "devil's gateway" to men. "How easily you destroyed man, the image of God!" shouts Tertullian at all women. "Because of the death which you brought upon us, even the Son of God had to die."

In our own Christian communities, women have often suffered the indignity of not being taken seriously. A Christian college student is referred to by one of her professors as a "cute little number." Some-

Questions about Humanity

one's grown-up wife is introduced as "the little woman." People gather to discuss "the women's issue," and men do all the talking. Churches meet in their annual conventions and men discuss with other men what privileges they might be persuaded to grant to "their" women.

However we understand what the apostle Paul says about male headship in marriage, his radically new teaching about our general relations as male and female is that in Christ males and females are *one*. Gentiles have been liberated from secondary status to Jews! Slaves have been liberated from secondary status to masters! And women have been liberated from being the property of male fathers and the incubators for male children! Jesus Christ came to "set at liberty those who are oppressed," and his liberty is cultural as well as spiritual. Christ came so that as male and female we may have life, and have it in its fullness.

Faithful God, we confess our uneasiness with the deepest implications of your Word. We confess our puzzlement with your Word itself, which seems in our deafness and confusion to speak with more than one voice. Guide us by your Holy Spirit to hear what you are saying to us. Then give us the courage to do it, through Jesus Christ our Lord. Amen.

Male and Female: How Are We Related?

53

> *So God created humankind in his image, in the image*
> *of God he created them; male and female he created*
> *them. God saw everything that he had made, and in-*
> *deed, it was very good.*
>
> GENESIS 1:27, 31

As male and female we are one in Christ. But we have also been equipped by God to become one flesh. We are related as *sexual* creatures. God has made a way for us to know each other with the deepest intimacy, a way for us to know a part of each other's mystery. Do we dare say, "This is the way the Lord has made! Let us rejoice and be glad in it"?

The church fathers did not dare say it. Some thought husbands and wives ought to abstain from sex if possible, or else blush in the morning. Many Christians still find it hard to rejoice in their sexuality. They underestimate sex. They think it's not nice. Or else they regard it as a duty. Some, pressured by high-powered jobs or by multiple demands on their energy, bracket their sexual nature. They just don't have time for it.

All this is a mistake. Why despise or neglect what God has made and what God calls good? Why forget that our maleness and femaleness allow us to express the very image of God? I'm not saying that God is male or female. I'm saying that sexual union allows us to reflect something of the profound communion among the persons of the Holy Trinity. Sex is the gift that drives us toward the other:

> We want to experience the other, to trust the other . . . to enter the other's life. . . . Personal communion is what the image of God is about.
>
> *(Sex for Christians)*

But sex, like fire, is a powerful gift that not only can draw us to its warmth but can also burn us. There is delight in sex. Surely there is humor in it. Sometimes sex is a romp. But sex for Christians, even when it is a joy, is not a toy. We do not play with fire. Sex needs a context. It needs a *fireplace*. Because it has power to uncover our inadequacies and to explore our tender places, sex needs to be guarded by the security of that life-union we call marriage.

We are sexual creatures. We must not underestimate either the joy or the power of sex. This great gift can light up two lives, or it can turn them, for a time, to ashes.

O God, you are strong to save. In sex as in all else, create a new and right spirit within us and restore to us the joy of our salvation. Through Christ, Amen.

Male and Female: How Are We Related?

54

132

Train yourself in godliness, for, while physical training is of some value, godliness is valuable in every way, holding promise for both the present life and the life to come.

1 TIMOTHY 4:7-8

Errors come like shoes — in pairs. Take physical fitness. Two generations ago any middle-aged man (let alone a middle-aged woman) who tried to swell his lungs and shrink his paunch by running around outdoors, or by lifting weights, would have been thought peculiar. After all, only professional body builders lift weights. Only kids run around. Grown-ups are supposed to *sit* around, growing large and soft.

Now all has changed. For some people, fitness is a religion. According to them, bodily training will raise up every valley and lay low every mountain in your life. So these folk buy their outfits and strut their stuff, trusting exercise to make them well.

Against both errors Paul writes to Timothy: "Train yourself in godliness, for, while physical training is of some value, godliness is valuable in every way."

Paul might just as well have been speaking of bodily sex. It is of some value, some *real* value. But it's not the most important thing in

Questions about Humanity

our lives! As Lewis Smedes says, the house has other rooms besides the master bedroom. We needn't adapt ourselves to an obsessed culture that pities virgins and grimly seeks the "atomic orgasm." This is a culture in which sex doesn't know its place, where people imagine that bodily sex can by itself create communion — only to find that when it does not express a prior commitment to life-union, sex plunges men and women deeper into emptiness.

We must not overestimate bodily sexuality. We do not have an unlimited right to fulfillment in it. Sexual sins are not the worst imaginable sins. And single people do not necessarily lack "wholeness" as persons. It is entirely possible to live a fulfilled and godly life without *bodily* sex. One of the ripest fruits of mature Christianity is the discovery that, married or single, we can enjoy each other *as male and female* without intending any movement toward a bed.

Even Adam and Eve had more to do in the garden than just cling to each other in the grass!

> *Help us once again, Lord God, to put first things first.*
> *Remove from us every nearsighted obsession with some*
> *single part of a gift you give. Turn us back to you, the*
> *giver, and to the widest possible vision of the richness*
> *we have as males and females. Through Jesus Christ*
> *our Lord, Amen.*

Male and Female: How Are We Related?

55

God has so arranged the body that . . . the members
may have the same care for one another. If one member
suffers, all suffer together with it; if one member is hon-
ored, all rejoice together with it.

1 CORINTHIANS 12:24-26

In one of his sermons Walter Burghardt tells a story of how a man and woman may care for each other. A surgeon had operated on a young woman, recently married, whose tumor had twined around a twig of her facial nerve. Despite the surgeon's great delicacy, he had cut the nerve. To remove the tumor, there was no other way.

Now the young woman's face looked a little clownish. When her young husband came into the room the couple began to deal with a postoperative fact: her mouth was now a kind of twist. The husband stood by his wife's bed, quietly dwelling with her in the lamplight. The physician observed the two of them making room in their love for a fact they had not wanted. And the physician reflected on the two of them, one with a solicitous manner and the other with a palsied mouth. "Who are these people?" he wondered. "The two of them gaze at each other so generously."

Questions about Humanity

The young woman speaks. "Will my mouth always be like this?" she asks. "Yes," said the surgeon. "It will. I had to cut the nerve."

She nods and falls silent. But the young man smiles.

"It's OK," he says. "It's kind of cute."

And all at once, as the surgeon witnesses the man and the woman together, he knows who they are. And he lowers his eyes because he is on holy ground. He lowers his eyes because "one must not be too bold in looking upon an image of God."

Then the young man "bends to kiss her crooked mouth," and the physician is so close to them now that he can see how the young man contorts his lips to fit hers. "What is he doing? *He's showing that their kiss still works.*" And the physician who had seen the mystery of two becoming one flesh — the physician takes a breath and lets "the mystery of this union come home."

We have all gotten used to caricatures of love. But when the caricatures have passed away, the real thing will endure because it is of God.

Dear Lord, fill us with your beauty so that we may seek to understand each other, even as we have been fully understood. In Jesus' name, Amen.

Questions about Jesus Christ

Question 12

How Do People See Jesus?

In contemporary Western society, nearly every thinking adult has an opinion about Jesus Christ. Millions of people faithfully believe Jesus to be the divine Son of God and the living Lord of their lives. Probably as many people believe only the first half of that confession: an astonishing number of people claim that Jesus is the divine Son of God but also that he, frankly, has little to do with their lives. Many, particularly in Europe, think of Jesus as a notable historical figure that others revere. And then there are those with peculiar, or even blasphemous, opinions about the identity of Jesus.

So far we have considered some questions about God and humanity. Now we turn to ask about the God-man, the divine person who, in the miracle of the Incarnation, became human for us and for our salvation.

We begin by asking a biblical sort of question: "Who do people say that I am?"

56

They went out and got into the boat, but that night they caught nothing. Just after daybreak, Jesus stood on the beach; but the disciples did not know that it was Jesus.

JOHN 21:3-4

To many people, Jesus Christ is a *remote* figure. Secularists shake their heads in disbelief when they hear Christians say they "love Jesus," "talk to Jesus," or have Jesus as their "friend." To such secularists, it's as if you said you loved a person from the planet Pluto, regularly spoke with him, and counted him among your kin! Incredible nonsense! Pluto is so remote that it can be seen only through the most powerful telescopes. And Jesus Christ died nearly two thousand years ago.

At times even some Christians view Jesus as a distant person. Liberal Christians who take a highly critical view of the Gospels say the early church made up most of Jesus' words and deeds. Jesus didn't really do the things the Gospels say he did. He didn't really say the things the Gospels say he said. Those things were said and done only by the "Christ of faith," an imaginary figure drawn into the Bible by the church's piety. The "real" Jesus, the "Jesus of history," is so remote as to be lost in the mists of time.

Questions about Jesus Christ

Some conservative Christians also think of Jesus as removed from us and all our littleness. These Christians think Jesus Christ is alive. But they think he is not, and has never been, really human. He's too lofty, too Christ-like. He never joked. He rarely sneezed. He never dropped a tool or bent a nail. Even as a boy, his knuckles were always clean. "The little Lord Jesus, no crying he makes." This Jesus is remote because he's unreal.

But the real Jesus Christ is as near to us as our own heartbeat. And he meets us not only in the churches, upper rooms, and sacred places of our lives. He also meets us where we are grimy and irritated. He meets us when we have gone fishing and caught nothing. The risen Lord elects to be with us where we live and sweat.

"Just after daybreak, Jesus stood on the beach; but the disciples did not know that it was Jesus."

God our Father, we have pushed away the one you meant to be with us. We have turned our backs on your Son, who has come to live with us. Now let Jesus stand on our beach, in our lives, where we work and play. In his name, Amen.

How Do People See Jesus?

57

> *He left that place and came to his hometown, . . . and*
> *many who heard him were astounded. They said,*
> *"Where did this man get all this? What is this wisdom*
> *that has been given to him? . . . Is not this the carpen-*
> *ter?"*
>
> MARK 6:1-3

To many people, Jesus Christ is a *familiar* figure. His picture hangs in the kitchen. His name is a household word. Songs about him — some of them sentimental songs — are played all day as a background to household tasks. Jesus is a "dear, familiar friend."

Even for some secularists, Jesus has become a familiar figure. They see him on the cover of *Time* magazine. Their own culture made him a superstar way back in the 60s. In some areas of the country, secularists are assailed on their car radios by Jesus preachers and confronted on their way to work by Christian billboards on which things of final magnificence are advertised alongside hotdogs and motor oil.

For many people — some of them teenagers in Christian homes — all this familiarity is not a delight but a burden. These people find it depressing. Their religious circuits are overloaded. They are overexposed. By turns, they are bored and rebellious where Jesus is concerned.

Questions about Jesus Christ

Even inside the Christian religion, familiarity can breed contempt. In fact, Jesus' own townspeople — those who knew him "back when" — could not honestly get very enthusiastic about him. Who does he think he is? "Where does he get all this? Is not this the carpenter?"

And isn't this all too familiar? What chance does Jesus Christ have among us when his gospel has to make its way through thick layers of religious familiarity? We have heard it all before. We have heard that name until it irritates us and the good news until it seems neither new nor good. There some of us sit, on the fringes of the church! "Go ahead!" we say. "Preach away! We know all the words. You aren't telling us anything!"

One of the most stunning displays of the power of Jesus Christ is that he can sometimes get himself heard even where people are numbed by years of sermons, hymns, and bumper-sticker piety. In some moment of unexpected need, the Word begins to speak. In a crisis sharper than we had thought possible, God's Son for the first time becomes real to us. It may happen when Peter's short prayer becomes ours: "Help, Lord!"

The familiar Jesus becomes a Savior. The resurrected carpenter becomes the Lord of life.

O Lord God, in some hopeless way, we have managed to make even the splendor of your Son seem dull. Forgive us. Startle us by your grace, surprise us by joy, and make all things new among us for Jesus' sake. Amen.

How Do People See Jesus?

58

[Jesus] asked his disciples, "Who do people say that I am?" And they answered him, "John the Baptist; and others, Elijah; and still others, one of the prophets."

MARK 8:27-28

Some people see Jesus as a remote figure; some see him as a familiar one. People have always been confused about his identity. During Christ's lifetime, people confused him with John the Baptist, Elijah, and Jeremiah. The scribes thought he was a lunatic. The soldiers thought he was a fool. The priestly crowd thought he was a robber. And his own disciples saw him as a political messiah.

We have all been tempted to twist Jesus into a shape fit for our own cause. We do not support *his* program; he supports ours. The silly-putty Jesus is the convertible idol of postmodern culture. He can be hitched to any chassis, packaged for any market, elected charter member of any group. We have all seen this sort of thing done with dismal regularity in our own day.

He can be arranged as a businessman (Didn't he say, "I must be about my Father's *business*"?). He was a Jesus for capitalists (didn't he say, "To everyone who has will more be given"?). But he can also be set up as a labor unionist (remember, he was a carpenter). Indeed, he was

Questions about Jesus Christ

the first real socialist (recall his warnings to the rich and his love for the poor). He can be packaged as a revolutionary, as a liberation theologian, and as the first pop psychologist and success preacher. He can be seen, and sung to, as a football player ("Drop-kick me, Jesus, through the goalposts of life!"). Some publishers of children's vacation Bible school materials feature a Hollywood-handsome Jesus peering out at us with his matinee-idol eyes.

People who have something to sell, something to hide, or something to prop up all want Jesus Christ as the patron saint of their cause. And Christians who watch such perversion will echo the ageless cry of Mary: "They have taken away my Lord, and I do not know where they have laid him."

O Lord Jesus Christ, Son of God, have mercy on me. O Lord Jesus Christ, Son of God, have mercy on me, a sinner. O Lord Jesus Christ, Son of God, have mercy on me and grant me your peace. Amen.

How Do People See Jesus?

59

Then the soldiers . . . knelt before him and mocked him,
saying, "Hail, King of the Jews!" They spat on him, and
took the reed and struck him on the head. After mock-
ing him they . . . put his own clothes on him. Then they
led him away to crucify him.

MATTHEW 27:27, 29, 31

A contemporary preacher tells of seeing one of those pieces of pious graffiti sometimes scrawled on walls and abutments. Someone had clambered up on a railroad bridge, far above the highway, to paint the words, "Jesus saves!" But someone else had risked life and limb too — someone who scrambled up there to add behind the motto the words "green stamps."

Certain people have always seen Jesus Christ as a fool. It's a wickedness we seldom call to mind. We think of the suffering Christ as grieved and hurt. We think of him as a tragic figure. Yet, as Douglas Nelson describes the scene from Matthew, here is the Christ draped with somebody's faded army blanket and crowned with the thorn's nest jammed down on his head. Bored soldiers try to get him into a game of blindman's buff. A good slap across the mouth: "Take it and

Questions about Jesus Christ

like it, your Majesty!" A fist to the nose: "Guess who gave you *that* one, O King!" "Hail, King of the Jews!"

The soldiers think they have a fool on their hands, and they think that's funny. But he's a Jewish fool, and that's not so funny. These soldiers are as anti-Semitic as an occupying force can be. They hate Jews and try to humiliate them whenever they can. Doesn't everybody know Jews are impossible to govern? Doesn't everybody know they're pushy and demanding? They're so full of chutzpah.

And here's one who takes the cake! Here's one who thinks he's a king! So, then, time for a little worship. "Hey, there, King of the Jews!" they shout at this silent man. "Yo! King of the Jews." Kike-King! Jew-King! In another cultural context they would have said "Nigger-King."

He was carrying our griefs and bearing our sorrows. And Matthew shows us why mockery is such a sorrow. "After mocking him, they . . . put his own clothes on him. Then they led him away to crucify him."

Where mockery is concerned, crucifixion is just a way of finishing it off.

> *O Christ our Lord, for the grief and shame that weighed you down we look to the weight of our own sin and the folly of our own hearts. Thank you for taking them upon you. Amen.*

How Do People See Jesus?

60

Then Jesus said to them, "Have you come out with swords and clubs to arrest me as though I were a bandit?"

MARK 14:48

As Ernest Campbell observes, this scene from Mark's gospel has a kind of grim humor. The crowd that snakes its way by torchlight through the garden to capture Jesus is ludicrously overarmed! You don't send out the FBI to trap someone who owes a library fine. And you don't approach the Prince of Peace, the preacher of nonresistance, with blades, bludgeons, and a show of muscle: "Have you come out with swords and clubs to arrest me as though I were a bandit?"

Every day he had been available to them. Every day he had freely preached in the temple. He was no fugitive. Why all this sudden and cowardly force?

Jesus, whose name means "Savior," has often been seen as a *robber.* People think he's out to steal our privacy, our riches, our freedom to do what we want. The poet Swinburne said it famously:

Thou hast conquered, O pale Galilean; the world has grown gray from Thy breath.

("Hymn to Proserpine")

Questions about Jesus Christ

To Swinburne, paganism is a rich and lush green world; Christianity is a tight and narrow little gray world. And the Swinburnes of the world have always wanted to set Barabbas free and eliminate the Christ.

A main obstacle to conversion is the fear that Christian faith will dry up our pleasures and leech all the color out of our lives. No more bright lights and good friends! No more lipstick! No more Miller High Life! Francis Thompson has it exactly:

> For, though I knew His love who followed,
>   Yet was I sore adread
> Lest, having Him, I must have naught beside.
>
> ("The Hound of Heaven")

Is Jesus Christ our robber or our Savior? Both. He carries off every false friend, every hopeless crutch, every deadly comfort. He means to rob us of life itself. But only of that old and dangerous life that leads to death. He wants to give us his kind of life — strong, purposeful, rich with love and joy. Perhaps it takes a veteran Christian to understand what Jesus meant when he said, "The thief comes only to steal and kill and destroy; I came that they may have life, and have it abundantly" (John 10:10).

> *O Jesus, joy of loving hearts, the fount of life, the light of men. From fullest bliss that earth imparts, we turn unfilled to you again. We turn unfilled to you again. Amen.*
> — TWELFTH-CENTURY LATIN HYMN

How Do People See Jesus?

Question 13

What Did Jesus Do?

Christianity, like Judaism, is a historical religion. The Old and New Testaments are testaments to great acts of God in history. Over and over, the pattern of relationship between God and his human creation is one of God's act and our response.

The New Testament tells us of the acts of God's Son, of the events of Christ. These are the events from incarnation through ministry, suffering, and death to resurrection, ascension, and present rule. They form the heart of the Apostles' Creed and the historical foundation of our faith. So now we explore in five different settings: What did Jesus do?

61

[He] emptied himself, taking the form of a slave, being born in human likeness.

PHILIPPIANS 2:7

For, behold, darkness shall cover the earth, and gross darkness the people; but the LORD shall arise upon thee, and his glory shall be seen upon thee.

ISAIAH 60:2 (KJV)

This year in Advent we will sing of "good news," and tell of "a great joy which shall come to all the people." We will do so in a season of the year in which depression deepens across the land and the traffic in suicide thickens.

"For, behold, darkness shall cover the earth, and gross darkness the people."

Even many Christians find a leaden familiarity in the old, old story and a seasonal slump in the good news. Together, they make Christmas uphill work. Where is the excitement we used to feel? What happened to the freshness of our childhood celebrations?

Well, thank God that faith does not depend on any joy that *we* manufacture. But with humility let's also thank God that here and there he

Questions about Jesus Christ

lets us feel again some of the wonder of his grace, which descends to lift up a desolate people. It's wonder, as Paul Scherer put it, at a God who "came one night down the stairs of heaven with a baby in His arms."

For many of us, a bass soloist can bring back the wonder and make our eyes sting as he sings from Handel's *Messiah:*

> For, behold, darkness shall cover the earth,
> and gross darkness the people;
> But the Lord shall arise upon thee,
> and his glory shall be seen upon thee.

Experts say that Handel was deeply depressed when he set out to write *Messiah.* But he also found himself profoundly moved by the texts for which he reached so deeply into his soul to find music. In fact, one story tells of a servant finding Handel in tears after he had just finished the "Hallelujah" chorus. He heard the composer whisper, "I thought I saw all heaven before me, and the great God himself!"

> For behold, darkness shall cover the earth,
> But the kingdom of this world is become the
> kingdom of our Lord and of his Christ;
> and he shall reign for ever and ever!

What did his Christ do? Did he arise upon us? He did, and he still does. But in the mystery of his way with us, Jesus Christ arises only after he descends on us. The wonder of Advent is wonder at the humility of the only natural Son of God who lowered himself into our darkness to bring every lost one of us to light.

> *O Holy Child of Bethlehem, descend to us, we pray.*
> *Cast out our sin and enter in; be born in us today.*
> *Amen.*
> — HYMN WRITTEN BY PHILLIPS BROOKS

What Did Jesus Do?

62

> *"Are you the one who is to come, or are we to wait for another?" And he answered them, "Go and tell John what you have seen and heard: the blind receive their sight, the lame walk, the lepers are cleansed, the deaf hear, the dead are raised, the poor have good news brought to them."*
>
> LUKE 7:20, 22

Classic Christian creeds often fall strangely silent about the life and ministry of Jesus. The Apostles' Creed, as E. A. Dowey remarks, locates the career of Jesus in the comma between "born of the virgin Mary" and "suffered under Pontius Pilate." The Nicene Creed does a similar thing. John Calvin's *Geneva Catechism* claims to find nothing of redemptive substance in the history of our Lord's life:

Minister: Why do you go immediately from His birth to His death, passing over the whole history of his life?

Child: Because nothing is said here about what belongs properly to the substance of our redemption.

Calvin must have been dozing at his desk! Our Lord's career has a huge impact on the substance of our redemption!

Questions about Jesus Christ

What did the Son of God come to do? He came to leave us "an example" that we should "follow in his steps" (1 Pet. 2:21). But more: "Christ Jesus came into the world to save sinners" (1 Tim. 1:15). But even more: he came to destroy the devil (Heb. 2:14) and to "disarm the principalities and powers" (Col. 2:15). But most of all, most broadly and cosmically of all, God sent his Son to unite or reconcile all things to him (Eph. 1:10; Col. 1:20). That is, he sent Christ to bring his kingdom near.

In his earthly life Jesus announced and demonstrated God's rule over individual human lives, over whole nations, and even over all of nature. In so doing, God's Son did not drop onto a vacant lot or into an anonymous nation. He was born as a particular Jew among Jews who had for centuries been looking for "the anointed one," the "expected one," the one whose coming would be accompanied by marvelous deeds in nature and human nature.

So John the Baptist sends out his question from "a depth not of years but of centuries." Has the troubled history of Israel come at last to that day when justice and peace would embrace? "Are you the one who is to come?"

And the answer comes back, heavy with the evidence that the anointed one, the *Christ,* has come at last.

What did Jesus do? By proclamation, miracle, prayer, and parable, he brought God's kingdom near.

You are the one, O Lord Christ. You are the promised one — and now the one who has fulfilled the promise. For this, and for all the splendor of your grace, we give you hearty thanks. Amen.

63

*When the days drew near for him to be taken up, he set
his face to go to Jerusalem.*

LUKE 9:51

Parents watch the faces of their children. Infants sometimes wear a
kind of counterfeit smile that really indicates only indigestion. Later
on the real smiles appear, the ones that light up a tiny face and much
of the room around it. Study an older child's face when she is sleeping
— a contented, peaceful face, oblivious to your presence. A face that
frowns as a cloud passes through the dreaming mind. The face of your
child.

"There's no art to find the mind's construction in the face," said
Shakespeare. Martin Luther claimed that a person's whole attitude toward God and humanity is written on his face and that, once past
thirty, a person is therefore accountable for the way his face looks.

No doubt Luther exaggerated. But you *can* tell something about
people by looking at their faces. Is the person sick? Look at that
peaked face. Is the person worried? Look at the frown and the tight set
of the jaw. Is the person old? Ashamed? Delighted? A face tells so
much that a skillful actress can generate the force of a whole scene just
by moving a few small muscles in her cheeks.

Questions about Jesus Christ

Now look at the face of our Lord, set like flint to go to Jerusalem. Every line on that determined face tells us that he is on his way to die and that he knows it. Nobody will take his life from him. He will lay it down. But the coming horror causes even the Son of God to grit his teeth. He will make detours, chat with the disciples, and reach out with divine love to nameless rascals. But always that steadfast look will be on his face. All the demonic forces are waiting up ahead. But all God's creation is waiting too — waiting for its redemption.

What did Jesus do? When the days drew near for him to be taken up, he set his face and he went to Jerusalem.

> *O Lord, we lack depth enough to take in your journey to the cross. Yet we know your wondrous love that moved along the way of sorrows for a whole world's redemption. We give you thanks. Amen.*

What Did Jesus Do?

64

Make a poisonous serpent and set it on a pole; everyone who is bitten shall look at it and live.

NUMBERS 21:8

I, when I am lifted up from the earth, will draw all people to myself.

JOHN 12:32

In John's Gospel, the cross of Christ exhibits a kind of shameful glory. There's no doubt of the shame. The religion of Golgotha centers, after all, on a homeless and crossed-out man. As Jürgen Moltmann once put it, this was a man crucified "not between two candles on an altar, but between two thieves in the place of the skull." Jesus, the friend of sinners, was crucified between his kind of people in the sort of god-forsaken place where you'd expect to find them.

And yet, almost unbelievably, the cross becomes a sign of God's glory. Jesus is *glorified* on these two-by-fours. He is lifted up by his crucifixion so that this howling wilderness event becomes, so to speak, the first ten feet of his ascension into heaven.

Think it over: exaltation on a cross. It's like being enthroned on an

Questions about Jesus Christ

electric chair. It's like being celebrated by a firing squad. Jesus Christ is lifted up like Moses' serpent, and in this horror the Gospel finds glory.

Of course the cross attracts its share of coarse persons for whom the death of God is a spectator sport — the sorts of people who like to munch popcorn at executions. But for all these centuries, people have also gazed at the dying Lord and found that they were pulled to him like a magnet. In awe these people see God at work. They see God sweating and straining to overcome human evil by suffering the worst of it, God emptying himself and taking on the form of a serpent so that whoever looks on him may live.

The central event in the Christian faith is obscene beyond telling: God in the hands of butchers. But even further beyond telling is a strange glory in the cross — a luminousness, a weightiness that no obscenity can smear. For in the gross darkness that falls across us from noon until three, the Son of Man arises on the earth. He is lifted ten feet above the earth to do the terrible work that casts such brilliant shadows over all that we have and all that we are.

The glory here lies in a love so fierce, so undignified, so determined that Jesus Christ is willing to be mocked and maimed and hung out there to suffer for the sin of the world.

Draw us, O Lord, to the terrible light of the cross. Rise on us so that your glory may fall on us. Amen.

What Did Jesus Do?

65

Pilate said to them, "You have a guard of soldiers; go,
make it as secure as you can." So they went with the
guard and made the tomb secure by sealing the stone.

MATTHEW 27:65-66

It is Saturday, the day between Good Friday and Easter, and the chief priests and Pharisees have not slept well. A particular thought has been nagging at them. What if Jesus' disciples take to grave robbing? What if they stage a "resurrection"? What if they recall the impostor's prediction that he would rise and conspire to fulfill the prediction themselves?

Off to Pilate they go to get a security order: "Command the tomb to be made secure until the third day; otherwise his disciples may go and steal him away, and tell the people, 'He has been raised from the dead'" (Matt. 27:64).

Pilate's answer is rich with a half-humorous, half-hopeless irony. "Go," he says, "make it as secure as you can."

"As secure as you *can!*" In one of his vivid sermons, Frederick Buechner pictures the helpless, bewildered look on the faces of these religious leaders. "As secure as you can. *But how secure is that?*" Are they, perhaps, secretly afraid not of a grave robbery but of something

Questions about Jesus Christ

else? Are they afraid the limp body might start to breathe again, might stand up and begin to move toward them unspeakably?

"As secure as you can." So many schemes and forces of unbelief have tried to secure that tomb against any outbreak of the Son of God. It's a shameful thing to admit that even some theologians have tried, in their own academic way, to tighten security in the area of the resurrection. It's not Jesus' body, they say, but his teachings that have been raised up to become immortal — like the art of Rembrandt and the music of Mozart. Or perhaps his historical impact lives on. Or, maybe, his Spirit still broods over our world as Lincoln's spirit still broods over Gettysburg. Or perhaps some of us can use our seminary training to wax eloquent at Easter about the return of spring to a winter's earth or the rebirth of hope in a despairing soul.

What the New Testament says is that Jesus arose. For all early Christian preaching and for all the centuries, this is the Gospel, the very core of the good news. On this bedrock fact all Christian faith, hope, and love are founded. The Son of God has gotten loose in the world, and no theologian will ever be safe again.

Go ahead! Make that tomb as secure as you can!

See what happens.

For the bursting of the tomb, O God, for the bursting of our worldly securities; for your amazing ways and amazing grace, we give you thanks, through Jesus Christ our Lord. Amen.

What Did Jesus Do?

What Is Jesus Doing?

Some Christians who "read that sweet story of old" about Jesus imagine what bliss it would be "to have been with him then." But was it always bliss to have been with him then? Certainly the Pharisees didn't think so. The rich young ruler didn't think so. Even Peter didn't think so. In any case, we were not with him then. We are with him now.

How? How is Jesus Christ alive and active in the world in this time between the coming of the kingdom and its final consummation? What is Jesus doing?

66

"These people who have been turning the world upside down have come here also and . . . they are all acting contrary to the decrees of the emperor, saying that there is another king named Jesus." The people and the city officials were disturbed when they heard this.

ACTS 17:6-8

The Christian church is boring even to some Christians. They hear lifeless, cliché-ridden, entirely predictable sermons. Their preachers are trained in safe, sleepy seminaries. Their congregations undertake only the most harmless and predictable ministries. Their church councils argue endlessly over small matters. Their worship services are endurance contests. Nothing is going on! There is no life here! No action! No movement! Somehow their church has lost the distinction between being founded on the rock of ages and being stuck in the mud.

To look from this modern boredom back to the first-century church is to experience culture shock. There we see our ascended Lord continuing his work by two means: his Spirit sent into the church and his church sent into the world. The disciples had been told to gather and "stay in the city" until they were "clothed with power." They did.

Questions about Jesus Christ

And one day the place was shaken. On Pentecost, Christ's body, his collective body, arose by the power of the Holy Spirit. The church began its movement through the world and across the centuries.

And look at it! The formerly timid disciples now speak with boldness. They are regularly beaten up and thrown into jail. Their mission has power, *dunamis,* dynamite! Modern Christians who yawn through their worship, who gird on their weapons to fight crabgrass on the church lawn, who live at a tiddly-winks level of faith can hardly understand why Christians should be seen as a threat! But the early Christians were. They were regarded quite literally as revolutionaries, as people who had "turned the world upside down."

Wherever we bow before "another king" than Caesar, wherever we are obedient to Jesus Christ, he is at work. It's not safe work. If we protest government corruption, subvert Hollywood propaganda, fight those who enslave the poor, challenge secularists on campus, expose child abuse, practice civil disobedience rather than sin against God, insist both on a day's work for a day's pay and also a day's pay for a day's work, send brave people out on unpopular missions — if we do these things, we will face trouble. Incidentally, some Christians today *are* doing these things. And they are not bored.

> *Creator Spirit, by whose aid the world's foundations first were laid. Come, visit every pious mind; come, pour thy joys on humankind; from sin and sorrow set us free, and make thy temples worthy thee. Amen.*
>
> — NINTH-CENTURY LATIN HYMN

What Is Jesus Doing?

67

So we are ambassadors for Christ, since God is making his appeal through us; we entreat you on behalf of Christ, be reconciled to God.

2 CORINTHIANS 5:20

Martin Luther King Jr. was one of the greatest Christians of the twentieth century. He was flawed. His theology left something to be desired. He had some troubling sins. Perhaps in these respects he resembled us. But who can hear his "I Have a Dream!" speech without being powerfully stirred? There was greatness in Washington that day! Of course, as a practicing Christian, King spent some of his time in jail. But who can read his "Letter from a Birmingham Jail" without being permanently convinced of the simple, elemental justice of his cause?

Martin Luther King Jr. was a prophet of the kingdom of God. He was an ambassador of the good news that the dividing walls of hostility have been broken down in Jesus Christ and that, in him, we are one. To white racists he said, "We beseech you on behalf of Christ, be reconciled to God." To black brothers and sisters bowed down by ignorance and crippled by poverty, he said, "In the name of Jesus Christ of Nazareth, stand up and walk!" King was a powerful man and, in many ways, a great apostle of the kingdom.

Questions about Jesus Christ

Jesus Christ first gathers his church and then disperses it across the world. From his own day, through the time of the apostles to the present, his rhythm remains. So we gather to hear the good news proclaimed. Then we fan out to proclaim it prophetically for every area of human brokenness, oppression, and sin. Christ the prophet is seeking to make his appeal through us. The New Testament verbs are all so insistent: "Go! Tell! Witness! Declare! Proclaim!"

And we, like some arctic river, are so often frozen at the mouth. "I fear the silence of the churches," said King, "more than the shouts of the angry multitudes."

Could it be that we will one day have to face those who were ruined by our silence?

O Lord our God, we confess the cowardice that has so often silenced us in the face of evil. Fill us with your Holy Spirit so that we may be bold in declaring your justice in all the reaches of our lives. Through Jesus Christ, who is still the Lord, Amen.

167

What Is Jesus Doing?

68

*You are a chosen race, a royal priesthood, a holy nation,
God's own people, in order that you may proclaim the
mighty acts of him who called you out of darkness into
his marvelous light. For to this you have been called,
because Christ also suffered for you, leaving you an example, so that you should follow in his steps.*

1 PETER 2:9, 21

Søren Kierkegaard, the Danish theologian, once published a work
called *Attack Upon Christendom*, a stinging rebuke of the state church
of Denmark for its lack of seriousness, for its degeneration into a social club. Kierkegaard complained particularly about the fact that
Christianity in Denmark was bland and effortless, while the Christians of the Bible faced peril and sword. When one sees a Christian's
life in Denmark, said Kierkegaard, how could one ever think that Jesus
Christ had said, "If anyone wants to come after me, let him deny himself, take up his cross, and follow me"? The ultimate outrage, he concluded, is to see fleshy, comfortable clergymen rising through the
ranks to softer and more luxurious positions, finally to stand beaming
as they are decorated with the cross. The *cross!*

Jesus Christ the priest carried his own altar through the streets of

Jerusalem and on toward the hill. Finally he mounted his cross and offered himself as a living sacrifice for all our sin.

He still serves the gathered church. The Christ who interceded with a high-priestly prayer for his disciples prays for us still, representing us before God in the manner of a priest. And every time we gather at his table, he nourishes and serves us with his resurrected life.

But the nourishment he offers is meant to make *us* priests. The church dispersed is "a royal priesthood" to represent all Christians before God and to pray that God may have his way with unbelievers, that God may forgive them, "for they do not know what they are doing."

The church is to bear the cross the world deserves, sharing in Christ's sufferings. We are to move as priests among those who suffer. We are to identify with them, cast our lot with them, suffer with them.

Only in so doing can we hold up their needs to God.

O Lord God, we confess that we have tried to lighten the cross of its awful freight. We have tried to plant our crosses in comfortable places. Now teach us to be priests to one another as your Son is to us. And make us priests to those whom no one cares to represent. Through Jesus Christ our Lord, Amen.

What Is Jesus Doing?

69

He answered, "I have been very zealous for the LORD, the God of hosts; for the Israelites have forsaken your covenant, thrown down your altars, and killed your prophets with the sword. I alone am left, and they are seeking my life."

1 KINGS 19:14

Even children know what an *epitaph* is. It's the bit of writing you find on tombstones. Some epitaphs are sad. Many are thoughtful. A few are disgruntled: "I told you I was sick!" "Here lies John Alfred Crane. My surgeon was Dr. Anthony Wendell."

For centuries unbelievers have been ready to write the *church's* epitaph. On some monument, perhaps at Rome, the world would write: "Outdated!" "Irrelevant!" "Outclassed!" "Finished."

Oddly enough, even some believers have been ready at times to follow suit. Here is Elijah, in our text, feeling lonesome and sorry for himself. He is complaining about the decline of the church. He wishes to point out that he has worked himself to the bone for the Lord, but everybody else has been tearing down what he has built. He has tried to lead, but nobody would follow. All the old breed are gone: "I alone am left." Everybody in the parade is out of step but me.

Questions about Jesus Christ

It's worth noting, as one modern preacher has said, that God gives Elijah not a pat on the head but a vigorous nudge. The management gives not a soothing word but a work order: Go, anoint two kings and one prophet to serve in your place.

In your place. The torch is handed on. In every generation our Lord renews his church with fresh prophets, priests, and kings. And every Sunday Jesus Christ arises in his body and moves out into the world.

So often the resurrection of the church comes by way of the command to get busy. Don't sit there feeling sorry for yourself and hankering for the good old days. Get to work! Preach the Gospel! Give your money away! Raise up a nursing home and two mental hospitals! Start a mission! Apply some pressure against political tyranny! Teach some children the truth!

In so many ways a renewed church can renew the world around it. Meanwhile, perhaps we will uncover at least seven thousand who never did bow the knee to Baal.

From our self-pity, O Lord, deliver us. From every deadly paralysis, rescue us. Then inspire us to be about your work in the world. Amen.

What Is Jesus Doing?

70

*He himself is before all things, and in him all things
hold together. He is the head of the body, the church; he
is the beginning, the firstborn from the dead, so that he
might come to have first place in everything.*

COLOSSIANS 1:17-18

Christians used to regard church discipline as one of the marks of the
true church. Not long ago discipline was both regularly practiced and
considerably feared. For many churches, that time seems to have
passed. One expert comments that in some cases today the membership standards of a boy scout troop are higher than those of the Christian church. But it's also true that some churches have recently *tight-
ened* their discipline in certain areas. For example, some churches that
used to be lax about the sin of racism now regard it as an offense that
should start the engines of discipline.

Jesus Christ the King is Lord of his gathered church. He governs
us by his Word and Spirit. And he disciplines us further by having us
hold *each other* accountable. Then he sends the dispersed church out
to discipline the society in which it lives — to guide it, to teach it, to
apply pressure to it, to hold it accountable.

Christians apply a number of social disciplines. Some work for tougher liquor laws, some for handgun control. Some argue for prayer in public schools; others want to open the public treasury to *all* legitimate schools, including Christian ones. In all such cases, the church is attempting to take what it regards as the will of God, or the mind of Christ, and reach with it into the world around.

But isn't Jesus Christ the Lord even *beyond* the reach of the church? Aren't there times when he "sets at liberty those who are oppressed" even when the church is nowhere in the vicinity?

Yes. The Spirit of Christ sometimes blows ahead of the gospel, and to wonderful effect. Wherever the walls of tyranny crumble, wherever age-old enemies sign a treaty and mean it, wherever old people are treated with respect, it happens because of the common grace of God and the secret work of Christ.

So the church needs the gift of discernment. Some worldly movements, judged by God's Word, must be opposed. But in other movements we will find the breath of the Holy Spirit. Then Christians will not fight the movement, but get with it and claim it for the Lord.

God of wisdom, let us test the spirits and find Christ where he works. Always govern us by your Word and Spirit so that we may honor Christ as Lord in every square inch of life. In his name, Amen.

What Is Jesus Doing?

Question 15

But Why Are
We Called Christian?

Theologians discuss the names and titles of Christ. Why is he called Jesus? Why Christ? Why Son of Man?

For the followers of Christ, those questions may remain comfortably abstract until they turn to address us. Jesus is called Christ because he is the anointed and expected one. But why are we called Christian?

The following meditations raise and answer the question five ways. But the answers, in turn, raise other questions that we may want to keep on pondering.

71

God . . . has anointed us, by putting his seal on us and
giving us his Spirit in our hearts as a first installment.

2 CORINTHIANS 1:21-22

If Christians had to list the four or five most exciting biblical ideas —
the ones most relevant to living as Christ's followers in today's world
— they might overlook the idea of anointing. Certain evangelical and
charismatic brothers and sisters have recovered the idea, but other
Christians don't know quite what to make of it.

Ancient people did a good deal of anointing. Much of it was
highly religious and ceremonial. But some of it was very practical. For
instance, people who lived in a desert would anoint themselves with
olive oil to keep their skin from drying out. Thus, the psalmist who
thanks God, for bread to strengthen his heart, and wine to gladden it,
does not forget to add his gratitude for "oil to make [one's] face shine"
(Ps. 104:15).

Today we don't go in for shiny faces quite so much. The only
Christians who still religiously anoint with oil are those who do it to
accompany prayers for healing, as described in James 5:13-16.

Still, we may be able to retrieve some of the force of Scripture for
today. Prophets, priests, and kings in the Old Testament were anointed;

Questions about Jesus Christ

that is, they had oil poured over them as a sign that God had called them to a particular office. In the fullness of time, the Messiah — the anointed one — was sent to perfect and finish the work of all three officers. Jesus Christ was anointed not with oil, but with water and the Holy Spirit. He was baptized.

And so are we. In baptism God claims us, marks us, sets his seal of ownership on us. When people are baptized, they are marked quite literally as secondary Christs, "anointed ones." In the church, the grace of God flows so freely as to anoint not only the head but also the whole body — not only the Christ but also the followers of Christ.

> *We acknowledge to you, O God, that you have marked us as your own. In your mighty love, empower us to bear Christ's name, live his kind of life, and do his work in the world. Amen.*

But Why Are We Called Christian?

72

There our captors asked us for songs, and our tormen-
tors asked for mirth, saying, "Sing us one of the songs of
Zion!" How could we sing the LORD's song in a foreign
land?

PSALM 137:3-4

In his novel *That Day Alone,* Pierre Van Paassen tells of the early years of World War II. One especially vivid incident offers a haunting parallel to the heartbroken question that comes at us from Psalm 137. Nazi storm troopers bring an elderly Jewish rabbi to their headquarters and begin to amuse themselves with him. While two of the troopers in the far end of the room slowly beat another Jew to death, the rabbi is stripped, beaten, and then ordered to preach the sermon he *would* have preached the next Sabbath if the Nazis had not destroyed his synagogue. He asks permission to wear his skullcap. His captors consent. After all, it adds another comic touch. So there he stands, naked, delivering his sermon on how God created human beings in his own image while the troopers grin and curse and hoot. Through it all, across the room the sound of clubs smashing into flesh and snapping bones goes on and on until it muffles itself in the silence of death.

"How could we sing the LORD's song in a foreign land?" Apparently, for the exhausted people of God camped in Babylon, the answer to that question was silence. They did not sing.

The question arises among us still. And we may not answer with silence. The New Testament insists that we tell the good news. We are from our roots a prophetic people. We may not keep the bread of life in a cupboard. Any song we have heard must be sung for others. Any gift we have received must be re-given. Let's say it straight out: If we do not confess Christ's name, we are not Christians.

But how do we do it? How do we do it in a land where secularism is the opiate of the people? How do we confess Christ's name in a culture where all the other world religions have *their* prophets? How do we speak of the finality of Jesus Christ to people who think it's arrogant to say *anything* is final?

"Jesus Christ" is the only name given under heaven by which people must be saved. Over the years we have learned how to say that name to each other.

But how do we sing the Lord's song in a foreign land?

> *Lord, speak to me, that I may speak in living echoes of your tone; as you have sought, so let me seek your erring children lost and lone. Amen.*
>
> — HYMN WRITTEN BY FRANCES R. HAVERGAL

But Why Are We Called Christian?

73

Then Jesus told his disciples, "If any want to become my followers, let them deny themselves and take up their cross and follow me. For those who want to save their life will lose it, and those who lose their life for my sake will find it."

MATTHEW 16:24-25

There once was a youth named Narcissus
Who thought himself very delicious
So he stared like a fool
At his face in a pool
And his folly today is still with us.

For a couple of decades North American people have been flirting with themselves. They find themselves fascinating. They chatter endlessly about the project of getting in touch with themselves (an indoor sport). They talk a lot about their feelings and about how they feel about their feelings. To some of these folk who define integrity as doing whatever they want, self-criticism is for Puritans. The self exists not to be disciplined, but to be expressed; not to be sacrificed, but to be fulfilled. In the same way that the church fathers judged pride,

Questions about Jesus Christ

some of our contemporaries judge self-denial: They think it's the first of the seven deadly sins.

Narcissus's folly is as old as the Fall. But it has not always been admired. People used to be ashamed of selfishness. No more. Even Christians are modulating to a major key in their song about themselves. Some big churches talk much less about the cost of discipleship than about its dividends. After all, these churches seem to say, if the Christian faith can't make us healthy, wealthy, and wise, what good is it?

Jesus talks a different language and preaches another gospel. He talks about counting the cost, about taking on his yoke, about self-denial, about losing our lives for his sake.

What does that mean? Shall we forfeit all our human rights and ignore all our own interests? Shall we become dumb sheep, waiting to be fleeced? Shall we cultivate a shabby self-image and learn to loathe ourselves? Shall we present ourselves to others as living doormats?

Not at all. Humility and great strength can go together. Insistence on our own rights and love for our neighbor can coexist. Self-sacrifice and self-assertion can dwell together. Self-denial and self-acceptance can join hands. Even losing one's life can be the road to finding it again.

How? "Those who lose their life *for my sake* will find it." For my sake. There's the key. And no doors open without it.

You, O LORD, are a shield around me, my glory, and the one who lifts up my head. Deliverance belongs to you, O LORD; may your blessing be on your people! Amen.

— FROM PSALM 3

But Why Are We Called Christian?

74

Just as Moses lifted up the serpent in the wilderness, so must the Son of Man be lifted up, that whoever believes in him may have eternal life.

JOHN 3:14-15

After nearly twenty centuries of Christianity, its main symbol is no longer terrible to us. We are not jolted by the sight of a cross, as we would be if we saw someone who wore a tiny electric chair around her neck. We domesticate the cross. We take it into our homes and lives, rounding its sharp edges, working it into our color schemes, learning to feel comfortable with it.

For some people the cross can become little more than a good-luck charm that accompanies wishing a wish or attempting a field goal. For some the cross is a decoration; they match its gold to their forest-green sweaters, or its lovely silver to their knotty pine walls.

But of course the cross was anything but lovely. There was no poise or decorum on a cross. Life on a cross was all shrieking and aching and ripping and writhing.

In a terrifying image, John's Gospel turns us toward Christ, writhing like a living snake nailed to a tree. The high-flying snake described in Numbers 21 has become a likeness of the crucified Lord. Christ the

Questions about Jesus Christ

snake must die so that whoever believes in him may live. This venomous death becomes our anti-venom.

How strange this is, that death can prevent death! It happens by what C. S. Lewis calls the "deep magic" that arises from the beginnings of time. Deep among the springs and roots of the universe is some mysterious fittingness that death should disarm death, that Christ the snake should crush the head of the serpent.

And, remarkably, faith in this Christ becomes a vaccine. By clinging to him, by identifying with him, we get inoculated with just enough of his death to produce a host of memory cells that circulate in the blood stream for years. These cells are primed to spring to the attack if ever we should be threatened by spiritual invasion or death.

Isn't this a wondrous dimension of human life? The spiritual immune system. Faith in the dying Christ produces in us a tiny edition of Golgotha, a little death that prevents big death. The best anti-venom turns out to be a small dose of the venom itself.

Who would have guessed it? Who would ever have figured that *this* is the way God saves?

O God, take away our safe cross, and lift our eyes to the hill from which our help comes. In Jesus' name, Amen.

But Why Are We Called Christian?

75

You have made them to be a kingdom and priests serv-
ing our God, and they will reign on earth.

REVELATION 5:10

One of the striking things about a great concert artist is that she's never completely satisfied with her performance. She may have performed a masterwork with power and precision — with what sounds to listeners like perfection itself. But she wouldn't necessarily agree. And she's not seeking refuge in false modesty; she really thinks she could have done better. She really thinks her best work only approaches the musical ideal.

We find the same sort of humility in science. The truly distinguished scientists are the humblest ones. They are deeply impressed with what a marvel this world is and how little we actually understand and control it. One celebrated scientist wrote a book in which he wonders at all the fuss over test-tube babies. After all, we have merely changed incubators. The real marvel, he says, is the joining of sperm and egg itself, and the cell that emerges — a cell that can grow into a human brain.

> The mere existence of that cell should be one of the greatest astonishments of the earth. People ought to be walking around all day, all

Questions about Jesus Christ

through their waking hours, calling to each other in endless wonderment, talking of nothing except that cell.

(Lewis Thomas, The Medusa and the Snail)

They would be talking about *creation,* about a wonder created out of the infinite resources of the mind of God. Creation and our dominion over it have been spoiled by the Fall. In many ways we are now powerless against the strength of flood waters, the sharpness of winds, the multiplying of cancerous body cells. Many times we can only wonder at nature — in awe or fear or both. Even in our own acts of creation, even in the cultural creation of arts, commerce, government, and education, our gifts are limited and our plans frustrated by sin. So often we are nature's victims and culture's captives.

But the whole Bible is whispering to us that one day we will be kings and queens over creation and creation's culture. Paradise lost will be regained. In the final age we will reign with Christ.

Not in the clouds. On earth. And not just for a thousand years. Forever.

> *Lord, you have been our dwelling place in all generations. Before the mountains were brought forth, or ever you had formed the earth and the world, from everlasting to everlasting you are God. Through Jesus Christ, Amen.*

But Why Are We Called Christian?

Questions about Our Salvation

How Are We Saved?

We have been asking about Christ our Savior. We move on now to ask questions about his salvation. Salvation, or deliverance, or reconciliation, is a broad and dynamic program of God to reconcile all things in Jesus Christ. To appreciate what God is up to in a fallen world, Christians try to keep a sense of the height and depth, the length and breadth, of God's salvation. Saving human souls is only one part of the program.

But it's a part we desperately need. And it's full of turns and surprises. In the next meditations, we'll explore some features of our salvation, including the continuing salvation we call "sanctification." Let's begin by asking how salvation comes to us. How are we saved?

76

I have uttered what I did not understand, things too wonderful for me, which I did not know. I had heard of you by the hearing of the ear, but now my eye sees you.

JOB 42:3, 5

190

Coming Home, a prize-winning film about the Vietnam War, portrays one of the most troubled times in the history of America. Vietnam was the first televised war. For people who sat in their family rooms, watching thatched villages being blown against the treetops, this war came home like no other. And, with an unspeakable hurt and sense of futility, for those who lost loved ones, the war came home in coffins and body bags. Years later that war and its misery still come home when we visit the Vietnam War Memorial in Washington, or see damaged veterans, or hear the stories of Vietnamese refugees. Even political campaigns sometimes center on the differences between those who went to Vietnam and those who did not.

Things that were once remote have a way of coming home to us. Not only bad things — terrorism, divorce, alcoholism, the environmental crisis — but also such good things as our parents' kindness in our youth, the charm and preciousness of our children, the graceful-

Questions about Our Salvation

ness of a strain of music we had heard a hundred times but which has just now come alive for us.

One of God's natural ways of saving human beings is by having them born or adopted into a Christian community. From early on, by word and example, these children are exposed to the truth. Children who are embraced in this living body can't help being marked with the fingerprints of Christ. Over and over such children discover by the "hearing of their ears" that life centers on Jesus Christ, his community, and on the reach of Christ's community to those who may be faithless or alone. Even when children do not say so, they are deeply influenced.

And one day a child who had been dedicated or baptized years before stands up before God's people to make an astonishing confession. To the Lord of whom he has heard so much for so many years, the child now says: "I had heard of you by the hearing of the ear, but now my eye sees you. O Lord, you have come home to me."

And the Lord says, "My child, so have you."

O Lord, for our own children and for children of the Christian community we pray. Help us to receive them in love, to care for their instruction in the faith, to encourage and sustain them in the fellowship of believers. And for all who have not yet come home, we ask your mercy. Now reach for them with an outstretched arm and bring them back for their own sake, and for the sake of Christ, your Son, who wants to gather us all in. Amen.

How Are We Saved?

77

Son, . . . we had to celebrate and rejoice, because this brother of yours was dead and has come to life.

LUKE 15:31-32

One young son left the home. One older son froze the home. It's hard to say which had been further from God. But it's easy to say which brother we church people relate to.

The older brother is our guy. He's the pharisee who thinks publicans will drag down property values. He's the laborer who works all day for a pay envelope no thicker than the one given to latecomers. He's the Sunday school boy who has stayed at home weaving potholders for refugees while also reading religious poetry to his mother. His younger brother has been sharing personal jacuzzis with exotic women; the older brother has been waiting his turn to use the Calvinist bathroom down the hall.

Predictably, the prodigal son's return gets the elder brother's undies in a wad.

What he resents above all is his father's amazing grace. For some reason his father isn't interested in getting even or in getting his money back or in shortening the prodigal's leash. Somehow the father isn't even very interested in the prodigal's confession. As Robert Farrar

Questions about Our Salvation

Capon tells us, the end of the story has nothing to do with a heart-to-heart talk in which God says to the prodigal, "Look, Sylvester. There is a little matter here of reestablishing your credit history so I can hold my head up in the village again."

Nothing like that. The end of the story is a hilarious party, a heavenly homecoming dance. This isn't a proper little after-church gathering over cookies and coffee. This is a feast. A neighborhood blowout, with music and hot food and dancing. *Dancing,* for heaven's sake.

And what about the sourball who objects to all this hoopla?

As Capon puts it, God has to explain to Mr. Respectability that the name of the game isn't bookkeeping any more. It's resurrection. The father says to the older brother, "Lighten up, Harold. Find the punch bowl, put on a funny hat, and come inside. Somebody you know has just come back from the dead."

One younger son left home. One older son froze the home. It's hard to say who had been further away from God. But it's also hard to measure the amazing grace that loves us at a distance — while we are still sinners — and calls for the dance to begin.

O God, your grace overflows like a fountain. In your presence is fullness of grace, plenty of grace, grace abounding forever. Through Jesus Christ, who journeyed into the far country for us, Amen.

How Are We Saved?

78

*The promise is for you, for your children, and for all
who are far away, everyone whom the Lord our God
calls to him.*

ACTS 2:39

John Newton, a former slave trader, wrote the lines of "Amazing
Grace" from great depths of shame and gladness. He says he once had
ambition like a Caesar. He was a hard man, a profane man, who
traded British manufactured goods for African slaves and then
packed those slaves like sardines in the hold of his ship. Newton's
journal tells us that he treated slaves as his enemies. But one night in
a storm at sea, the Holy Spirit began to blow, and got John Newton's
attention. One night the Holy Spirit got into John Newton's heart
and did Pentecost there, so that Newton began to speak in a new
tongue. What came out of his mouth were the words, "Lord, have
mercy on us."

"Lord, have mercy on us." Newton was calling on the name of the
Lord, and he got saved. The Pentecost promise is for all who are far
away — not just far away from Jerusalem, like the Romans way up in
the Northwest. No, as Thomas G. Long says, the promise is also for
those who are far away from God — the prodigal sons, the publicans,

Questions about Our Salvation

and a preacher at Pentecost named Peter, who once followed his Lord "from far away."

The promise is for people like John Newton, and so the Lord poured mercy into Newton — so much mercy into that man's hard heart that some of it flowed back out into the best-loved hymn in the English language. Newton knew that what's amazing about God's grace is not just that it flows to the undeserving; not just that it's so lavish and abundant. What's amazing about God's grace is that it can get through our armor and find our heart.

Jessye Norman, the great African-American soprano, speculates that the tune Newton used for his words was a tune he heard from his slaves. In God's amazing grace, a slave song became a freedom song. With this song, John Newton proclaimed Pentecost to the whole world. I once was lost, but now I'm found. Blind, but now I see.

And why? Because of the promise, of course. Because the promise of grace is for you, and your children, and for all who are far away.

Let your grace, O Lord, lift us like a tide. Let your grace lift us free of destructive pride and faithless fear. Hear us, O Lord. Amen.

How Are We Saved?

79

> *Judah said, "The strength of the burden bearers is fail-*
> *ing, and there is too much rubbish so that we are un-*
> *able to work on the wall." And I said . . . "Rally to us*
> *wherever you hear the sound of the trumpet. Our God*
> *will fight for us."*
>
> NEHEMIAH 4:10, 19-20

Someone has made up a wonderful story that extends both to heaven and hell. Sometime after Lucifer and his angels were exiled from heaven, the archangel Michael met Lucifer roaming around in outer space. Because of their old comradeship, they fell to talking. Michael asked what was the worst part of living in hell. And, with a wistfulness beyond telling, Lucifer said, "I miss the sound of the trumpets in the morning."

The gospel says that Jesus Christ has come to save sinners. God loves sinners and wants to give them grace. God loves people who are far away and wants them to come home. The business of the kingdom begins each day with this trumpet call. Faith is the instrument with which we are to answer that call.

Yet some Christians at times can't hear the call and can't find any faith to answer it. God doesn't appeal to them. Home doesn't sound

Questions about Our Salvation

good to them. Some feel guilty beyond all forgiveness; some feel anxious beyond all relief; some feel so spiritually depressed that they think even God can't lift them. They sin with a sinking heart, as St. Augustine once put it, and they know they're not *making* it!

"The strength of the burden bearers is failing."

Someone needs to speak a stout comfort to these people. Someone with strength and tenderness needs to tell these people that God loves them and that Jesus Christ suffered for them. Someone with the strength of God must pray for them when they can't pray for themselves, stand with them when they can't stand by themselves, grieve with them when grief is the only sign they are still alive. Someone with a faith that has known doubt and has then gone beyond doubt. Someone like Nehemiah: "Rally to us wherever you hear the sound of the trumpet. Our God will *fight* for us."

O LORD, my God, in you I take refuge; save me from all my pursuers, and deliver me. Through Jesus Christ, Amen.
— FROM PSALM 7

How Are We Saved?

80

He also told this parable to some who trusted in them-selves that they were righteous and regarded others with contempt: "Two men went up to the temple to pray, one a Pharisee and the other a tax collector."

LUKE 18:9-10

In one of his sermons Douglas Nelson pointed to the picture of guilt Shakespeare draws in the last act of *Macbeth*. Lady Macbeth, the icy, viciously effective woman who had nagged her spouse into becoming a murderer, now walks the corridors of the castle at night, sound asleep but never at rest. Her dreams keep taking her back to the night the two of them had slaughtered the saintly old King Duncan. Now, in her sleep, she keeps scrubbing at the red spots on her fingers, the blood that will not go away. Over and over she mutters, "Who would have thought the old man had so much blood in him?"

Lady Macbeth is not suffering from a failure of human relational adjustment dynamics. She is suffering the effects of *sin*. Her problem is not a guilt-neurosis. She is *guilty*.

Lady Macbeth and her guilt, Martin Luther and his agony of con-science, our own ancestors and their religious fear of the wrath of God — all these are almost incomprehensible to a certain sort of contem-

Questions about Our Salvation

porary Christian. For some of us, at least at some times in our lives, our problem with faith is just the opposite of the one we saw in the last meditation. We don't despair of salvation; we presume it. We don't worry too much; we worry too little. We don't say, "I'm not making it!" We say, or at least we feel, that we've made it big. We're in. We're in like Flynn. It's God's job to forgive; our job to enjoy forgiveness. So let the little people lose sleep over their sins.

For people who trust God, a sense of security is God's cradle of grace. But for people who "trust in themselves that they are righteous," a sense of security can become a trap. The New Testament has a dark strain in it about those who trust in themselves. The danger is that one day their trap will spring shut with heaven's coldest words: "I never knew you."

Faith is the gift with which we grasp God's grace. God's *grace!* Grace is not God's applause for the comfortable. Grace is God's long reach for sinners who are far away.

O Lord God, comfort the afflicted and afflict the comfortable among us. Teach our hearts to fear — and then relieve our fears through Jesus Christ our Lord. Amen.

How Are We Saved?

Question 17

What Do We
Expect from Salvation?

Some people expect very little from salvation, and they get it. They expect God's salvation to cure a few of their bad habits and to help them live more decently. They expect to be able to believe the right doctrines without raising any question about them. And they expect God to be night watchman over their possessions until they die and go to heaven.

Others seem to expect too much — or, at any rate, too much too early. These are people who expect sinlessness or the wealth of heaven or rest from their labors or unceasing ecstasy. They want glory now.

What do we expect from salvation? Hidden in that question is another: What should *we expect?*

81

A man lame from birth fixed his attention on them, ex-
pecting to receive something from them. But Peter said,
"I have no silver or gold, but what I have I give you; in
the name of Jesus Christ of Nazareth, stand up and
walk."

ACTS 3:2, 5-6

Charles Dickens wrote a novel about a young man with *Great Expecta-*
tions. This young man expected money. He ended up with happiness
instead.

In the incident recorded in Acts, Peter and John face a similar
man at the temple. Like a veteran bellhop or waiter, the man has
doubtless become an expert at sizing people up. This one will give a
dollar. That one will be good for more. This one is good for nothing.

The lame man "fixed his attention on them, expecting to receive
something from them."

Well, you know the famous response with its wonderful irony. "I
have no silver or gold, but I give you what I have." The man's heart
must have sunk like a stone. He was going to be handed a tract instead
of a meal. He had heard it all before: "I don't want to part with any of
my money — but God bless you."

Questions about Our Salvation

The man actually received a gift far greater than he had asked. He expected money. He got a miracle.

That miracle is still needed. God's salvation promises divine forgiveness and acceptance. It promises us a new status with God. Somehow people keep expecting things like money or power instead. Somehow they keep expecting *worldly* status. In fact some preachers inflame that expectation.

It's a big mistake. Salvation does not promise us material wealth — at least not for now. And it's a good thing. For when people fix on wealth as their main comfort, their attention wanders away from Jesus Christ. It also seems to wander away from needy brothers and sisters.

According to an old story, the pope stood one day with Erasmus outside the gates of the Vatican. A long line of horse-drawn carts creaked past them, loaded with the annual income of the church. A regiment of soldiers with drawn swords and cocked crossbows guarded this parade of treasures. The pope turned to Erasmus and said with satisfaction, "No longer can the Holy Church say, 'gold and silver have I none.'"

Erasmus answered very quietly, "No. Neither can it now say to the lame, 'Walk.'"

> O Lord our God, we have looked for riches, which would corrupt us. We have wanted human approval more than yours. And we have expected you to guard our worldly goods. Forgive us, we pray, and take us back to Christ and to the least of his brothers and sisters. Amen.

What Do We Expect from Salvation?

82

Jesus said to them again, "Peace be with you. As the Father has sent me, so I send you."

JOHN 20:21

One of society's miseries, judging from the drug traffic backed up across the Northern Hemisphere, is anxiety. People feel uptight. So they smooth out their lives by bottle, needle, or pill. For hopeless crackheads in urban shooting galleries, jittery professionals on suburban business campuses, restless teens in every high school in America, there are modern peddlers of peace. The peddlers do business in cocaine, Valium, and lemon vodka. These are the prophets who shout "Peace, peace!" where there is no peace.

What they're selling is escape. They're selling a kind of float-trip:

How sweet it were, hearing the downward stream
With half-shut eyes ever to seem
Falling asleep in a half-dream!
    (Alfred Lord Tennyson, "The Lotos-Eaters")

As the tragedy of addiction tells us, false prophets promise false comforts. People want peace, choose the wrong pacifier, and end up

Questions about Our Salvation

avoiding their lives. What's tragic is not just what addicts do to themselves and others; it's also what they miss.

"Peace be with you," says Jesus. "As the Father has sent me, so I send you."

Salvation offers us release from our burden of guilt, rest for our restlessness, and wholeness for all the bits and pieces into which our lives crumble. In some deep and wondrous way the Christian faith offers a peace that "passes understanding."

But it's not a sedative. In the same breath Jesus talks about peace and then about *sending*. And we recall, somewhat uneasily, that the Father sent his Son not to be served, but to serve. Jesus made peace only "through the blood of the cross."

The disciple is not greater than his master. For us too there is a cross to take up, a race to run, a fight to win. Strange to say, the peace we are given is a peace we take into battle. The peace of Christ is not for escape, but for survival. And, at the end of the day, for true comfort.

> *O LORD, bless us and keep us. Make your face to shine upon us and be gracious to us. Lift up your countenance upon us and give us your peace. Amen.*
>
> — FROM NUMBERS 6

What Do We Expect from Salvation?

83

As for mortals, their days are like grass; they flourish like a flower of the field; for the wind passes over it, and it is gone, and its place knows it no more.

PSALM 103:15-16

These words from Psalm 103 are among the most haunting in all the Bible. Usually they find their way into the readings at a funeral, and with good reason. The words say what impresses every reflective human being who pauses at a milestone. The words tell us that human life is brief.

The career that begins in diapers and moves on through the years of strength, on into the ripe old years when a person slows, turns, and looks back — that career seen from near its end seems so short. One day the body that has been a moving temple of the Holy Spirit can move no further. Finally, the Lord whom we seek suddenly comes to his temple and reaches for us.

"Like grass!" says the psalmist. A blade of grass sprouts and pushes its way up among all the other young blades. And one day a good sharp wind lays it low, and it's gone. Or, "like a flower!" Once, in this place, among these trees and hills, a person flourished — a person with roots, growth, color, complexity, and a unique sort of beauty. But now nobody remembers her. Her place knows her no more.

Questions about Our Salvation

People are born; they toil and die. Generations of people. What is the meaning of this passing of the generations? Poets and philosophers have reflected on the fleetingness of human life, which is here and then gone. What does it mean? Where have all the flowers *gone?*

Consider two answers. One of them is found in Shakespeare's words:

Life's but a walking shadow, a poor player
That struts and frets his hour upon the stage
And then is heard no more: It is a tale
Told by an idiot, full of sound and fury,
Signifying nothing.

(Macbeth)

The other answer begins the same way: "As for mortals, their days are like grass." But then it goes on: "Its place knows it no more. *But the steadfast love of the* LORD is from everlasting to everlasting on those who fear him" (Ps. 103:15-17).

The only meaning our lives will ever have is a meaning conferred by that everlasting love. This is the love that has planted the generations, cultivated them, and kept them. This is the love that one day comes not as a grim reaper to cut us down but as a faithful husbandman who wants to transplant his trees to a place where their leaves can be "for the healing of the nations."

O God, our help in ages past, our hope for years to come, still be our guard while troubles last, and our eternal home. Amen.

— HYMN WRITTEN BY ISAAC WATTS

What Do We Expect from Salvation?

84

And while my glory passes by, I will put you in a cleft of
the rock, and I will cover you with my hand until I have
passed by; then I will take away my hand, and you shall
see my back; but my face shall not be seen.

EXODUS 33:22-23

Moses is like us. At times he is close to God, filled to the brim with God. And at other times he feels as if God's presence in him has dried up. Moses has been on the mountain with God. But he has also struggled through some valleys.

One day Moses grows tired of these spiritual dips. He wants to be done with his questions and uncertainties. He wants God to come out of hiding. He wants to see all there is of God and to see it now. He wants the full-strength dose.

Moses says, "Show me your glory, I pray."

We understand his interest. As Jonathan Edwards said, "True religion consists in great measure in the fervent exercises of the heart." And what would get our hearts going if not a vision of the glory of God? Show me! says Moses. Let me taste your sweetness and see your brightness. Show me!

But God slips past Moses' request, which reminds us that God

Questions about Our Salvation

may be known, but God is also hard to know. God does reveal himself, but by grace, not on demand. O God, prayed St. Augustine, "you are deeply hidden and most intimately present."

Hungering and thirsting for God is a believer's natural appetite. But it is possible to become a spiritual glutton who wants heaven now. Private revelations from the Holy Spirit! Rapture around the clock! Visions, voices, prickly flesh, heavenly razzle-dazzle! Fireworks in our faith!

Perhaps it's wise to remember that the fruit of the Spirit includes not only love and joy, but also patience and self-control. God knows how much glory we need. God will not fill our teacups with a fire hose. "Show me your glory!" says Moses. And God shows Moses his "back." It was enough. And, one day, to disciples begging to see the Father, Jesus Christ said, "The one who has seen me *has* seen the Father."

The glory of God in the face of Jesus Christ.

You, O God, are deeply hidden and yet most intimately present. You are both veiled and unveiled. By your grace, show us your glory where you choose to reveal it, in the face of Jesus Christ your Son. Amen.

What Do We Expect from Salvation?

85

Therefore, keep awake — for you do not know when the master of the house will come, in the evening, or at midnight, or at cockcrow, or at dawn.

MARK 13:35

One last word about our expectations. These five meditations edge us toward the conclusion that God's salvation is often surprising. God comes when we least expect him, from a direction in which we are not looking, and in ways we don't always welcome. God's ways are not our ways.

It has always been so. Saul hoped to go to Damascus to rescue God's people from the people of "the Way." He was ambushed by Jesus Christ. Peter wanted to preserve salvation for those with clean hands and kosher habits. He was disturbed by a broader vision. For centuries God's people longed and hoped for a mighty warrior in David's line who would come to sit on their throne. One night the Son of God slipped into the world in a cave.

It still happens. In places where nobody sings hymns or wears good clothes. In places where most of the words come to about four letters. Even in the power places where humility is forbidden and kindness is a sign of weakness. One of the most improbable of every-

Questions about Our Salvation

thing that came out of the Nixon White House was a set of Christian conversions, including the conversion of Charles Colson, who has silenced his critics with a powerful life of service to prisoners.

Whittaker Chambers started on the road to faith by noticing the design of his daughter's tiny ear. But there was another step in his conversion. As Douglas Nelson tells it, Chambers remembered a girl in his grade school. She was red-faced, raw-boned, foul-tongued, and violent. The boys called her filthy names and loved to badger her into kicking and cursing. One day at lunchtime Chambers looked into a classroom and saw "Stew-Guts" (which was one of the more printable names for her) patiently drilling her little sister in spelling. The little sister was slow to learn, and had trouble with even the simplest words. But over and over the ugly girl took the little one through the words. Then, when the bell rang, Stew-Guts gently kissed her sister on the head and sent her off to her room.

The flicker of God's grace in unexpected places can save a human soul.

Watch therefore — for you do not know when God's salvation may come. Not at the end. Not even now.

> *In our blindness, O Lord, we have missed the signs of your presence. You have been working in places where we were not looking. Open our eyes to see, our hearts to receive, and our lives to show the great salvation you work through Jesus Christ our Lord. Amen.*

What Do We Expect from Salvation?

Question 18

What about Sin?

A cliché is an idea or expression that has lost its force and freshness through overuse. Some clichés are single: a grain of salt. Others are double clichés: rack and ruin. Some clichés get foolishly mixed by the unwary: It was as easy as a bump falling off a log.

    A cliché often shows verbal deftness or contains some real wisdom. That's why it is used so often. That's how it became a cliché. So it is with Christian clichés about sin. Following The Book of Common Prayer, *Christians have for centuries asked God's forgiveness for sins of "omission and commission" and for those of "thought, word, and deed."*

86

If we say that we have no sin, we deceive ourselves, and the truth is not in us.

1 JOHN 1:8

Why do some spouses miss all the signs of their spouse's infidelity? Why do alcoholics and other drug abusers typically go through years of denying their problem? Why is the revelation of incest an astonishment to people who are living right in the middle of it? How do adulterers convince themselves that all the wreckage in their wake is really temporary? Why do battered women go back again and again to brutal men who keep insisting that each incident is the last?

"We deceive ourselves, and the truth is not in us." In particular, we deceive ourselves about our sin.

Do we sin in spite of ourselves? Do we always have good intentions? Are our sins usually accidents? Are we generally at least *aiming* right when we miss the mark? Are we bewildered by our sin — like Aaron who was dumbfounded by the way his golden calf just popped into existence? ("Of all things! Imagine my surprise!") Do we "fall into sin" as a blindfolded party guest stumbles into a swimming pool?

No. We deceive ourselves. Let's face the truth. At times even redeemed people purposely plunge themselves into sin. In fact, we use a

Questions about Our Salvation

diving board. We go in head first, eyes wide open. We *commit* sin. And we often like it. Half-desperate or merely rebellious, we go after the pleasure we think some sin will bring. Sometimes we even take pride in a particular sin and try to defend it. Can we honestly say we have never relished putting down another human being — and then defended the put-down by claiming that the person "had it coming"?

We sin. We *commit* sin. And sin is no joke. The memory of our sins of commission is not the occasion for a wink or a shrug or a cocktail-party reminiscence. Sin needs confession. And confession of sin is like taking out the garbage. Once is not enough.

If we say that we have no sin, we deceive ourselves and the truth is not in us.

> *You desire truth in the inward being, O God. Therefore teach me wisdom in my secret heart. Hide your face from my sins, and blot out all my iniquities. Through Jesus Christ, Amen.*
>
> — FROM PSALM 51

215

What about Sin?

87

Then they also will answer, "Lord, when was it that we saw you hungry or thirsty or a stranger or naked or sick or in prison, and did not take care of you?"

MATTHEW 25:44

216

Thomas Muenzer, one of the more colorful figures of the Protestant Reformation, regarded Martin Luther as a half-baked reformer. He criticized Luther not for his beer drinking, but rather for drinking beer while he should have been working harder for reform. He called Luther "Professor Easy-Chair" and "Dr. Pussy-Foot."

Sins of omission are easy to see in others. And they are very real in others. More than one mission has failed because no one could be budged out of an easy chair to do it. More than one ministry to the hungry, the old, or the imprisoned has foundered because Christian people were simply indifferent. More than one family of children has grown up starved for a father's love because the father omitted to love them. We see such omissions in others and wonder why *they* don't see them.

Sins of omission are harder to see in ourselves. And yet they are very real. One of Christ's most disturbing teachings is that you and I will be judged not merely for what we have done, but also, maybe par-

Questions about Our Salvation

ticularly, for what we have not done. We will be asked about those things we never did — perhaps, as C. S. Lewis remarks, about those things "we never *dreamed* of doing." It's a sobering thought that the heaviest charge against any one of us may be the charge that we were unconcerned.

Someone's need was at our door, and we preferred to watch television. A call went out to begin a prisoner-visiting program, and we answered the call to start a golf league. Someone wrote a troubled letter, and we never answered. A cancerous relative was dying, and we were too timid to visit. Another student at school was unpopular and unhappy, and we tried not to notice. Our whole nation pointed itself toward destruction, and we didn't even bother to vote.

Of course, we could always plead ignorance. On the last day we could say, "Lord, *when* did we see you hungry or thirsty or in prison?"

But how good an excuse is that?

O Lord Christ, we come to you for mercy. Forgive those things we ought to have done and did not do. Soften our hearts and ready our hands to do your work. Amen.

What about Sin?

88

Search me, O God, and know my heart; test me and know my thoughts. See if there is any wicked way in me.

PSALM 139:23-24

The psalmist prays to an inescapable God. We can shield our thoughts from each other, but not from God. We can hide our shame, but not from God. We can outsmart our competitors, but nobody outsmarts God. Even death brings no escape. People who hope to "end it all" discover God on the other side and have to face him again.

It can make a person crazy. Everywhere we go, God is already there. Even inside our own brain, there is God. We always have company. We never have privacy. God is always before us, and (as Paul Tillich wrote) this is why people always try to kill him. Our Savior ended up on a Roman cross because he brought God much too close.

What this means is that our sinful thoughts are known. Many twenty-first century people think that the only sinful thought one can have is a bigoted thought. All else is your own business — maybe even bigotry if you keep it to yourself.

The truth is more scandalous. All the root sins are thoughts: arrogance, envy, malice, greed, boredom with God, twisted desire of one

Questions about Our Salvation

kind or another. They might show up as words and deeds, or might not. But they mark our character and shape our destiny. And God knows them.

This would be nothing but terror if it weren't for the perfect love of God shown in the cross and resurrection of Christ. Nobody but God can know our thoughts and still love us unconditionally. We ourselves find it tough to know our thoughts and still hold our heads up. But to be known through and through by perfect love is a comfort. To paraphrase Philip Yancey, nothing I can think will make God love me more; nothing I can think will make God love me less.

O Lord, you have searched me and you know me. From my first day you have overshadowed me. You know, O Lord, not only what I say, but also what I almost said. You know not only what I do, but also what I wanted to do. You know when my pride makes me swell, and you know when my shame makes me shrink. O Lord, you are familiar with all my ways, and you love me still, through Jesus Christ. Amen.

89

From the same mouth come blessing and cursing. My brothers and sisters, this ought not to be so.

JAMES 3:10

G. K. Chesterton once remarked that some people will try to end an argument by saying, "We're only quarreling over words." But words are *worth* quarreling over, said Chesterton.

> Why shouldn't we quarrel about a word? What is the good of words if they aren't important enough to quarrel over? Why do we choose one word more than another if there isn't any difference between them?
>
> *(The Ball and the Cross)*

Chesterton is right. Think of the difference between saying "You're kidding!" and "You're lying!" Think of the difference in shading between "steadfast" and "stubborn," between "good" and "goody-goody," between "wise man" and "wise guy."

Words matter. Sticks and stones may break my bones — but words may break my heart. Many of us know this from painful experience. A group of children mocks a loner, and the picked-on child

Questions about Our Salvation

wants to die. A parent tells a teenager that she's a tramp, or that he's a loser, and the words stick in memory. A husband says, "I never did love you," and a wife feels whole decades unraveling. Curses are like biblical blessings: once they're out of your mouth you can't get them back.

Gossip, curses, slander — bad words that do bad things. But, as we have seen before, our silence can be just as dangerous: the encouraging word never said to a struggling daughter; the grateful word withheld from an aging parent; the prophetic word silenced by self-righteous pieties. Sometimes we simply omit to say thanks to God for his mercies, which are new every morning.

James knew the power of the tongue for good and for ill. "From the same mouth come blessing and cursing," he said. "My brothers and sisters, this ought not to be so."

221

> Let the words of my mouth and the meditation of my heart be acceptable to you, O LORD, my rock and my redeemer. Amen.
> — FROM PSALM 19

What about Sin?

90

*The saying is sure and worthy of full acceptance, that
Christ Jesus came into the world to save sinners — of
whom I am the foremost.*

1 TIMOTHY 1:15

Sins of omission and commission, thought, word, and deed, are a continuing presence in the lives of God's people. Partly because of society's attitudes, we live with them too easily.

An armored car once lost two bags of money near Trenton, New Jersey. Perhaps it had a leaky door. An unemployed worker found the money. It was a great deal of money, hundreds of thousands of dollars. Being an honest man, the worker returned the money at once to the armored-car company.

The company was grateful to this honest man. It gave him a reward of a thousand dollars.

The man was not grateful for the thousand dollars. He was honest, but not grateful. He told reporters it should have been far more. "Is that all honesty is worth?" he demanded. "A lousy thousand bucks? Why that hardly bought my gas to *return* the money!"

No doubt this man underestimated his car's fuel efficiency. And later he apologized for his ingratitude. But his first reaction was inter-

Questions about Our Salvation

esting because it took crookedness as the rule and honesty as the exception. You used to hear about people refusing a reward — saying they had simply done their duty. They had simply done what anybody would do. Nowadays people sometimes think honesty is a foolishness so far beyond the call of duty that it deserves a ceremony. And a hefty check!

One of our continuing problems as Christians is that we live in a pocket of history where, as C. S. Lewis has it, "mere decency passes for heroic virtue and utter corruption for pardonable imperfection." These attitudes rub the good, sharp edges off our conscience. The trouble with a rubbed-off conscience is that it can no longer detect the depths of sin or the heights of grace.

The apostle Paul called himself the "foremost of sinners." He meant it. He had developed *sensitivity* to sin. Saints know their sins of thought, word, and deed. They also know that Jesus Christ died to save sinners.

> *O Almighty Father, Lord of heaven and earth, we confess that we have sinned against you in thought, word, and deed. Have mercy upon us, O God, after your great goodness; according to the multitude of your mercies, do away with our offenses and cleanse us from our sins, for Jesus Christ's sake. Amen.*
>
> — FROM THE AMERICAN
> BOOK OF COMMON PRAYER

What about Sin?

Question 19

How Should We
Handle Our Wealth?

One of the most sensitive questions in a capitalist society is the question of money. You are either a "success" or you are not. Indeed, with little sense of irony, our society uses words like "successful" and "well-to-do" with an almost exclusively financial reference.

Not too long ago Puritans and other Christians saw wealth as worldly. But we are getting more liberal. We now have wealth ourselves, and it no longer seems so worldly. And yet, we can't rid ourselves of a troubling and biblical question: What does God want us to do with our wealth? If we are "saved to serve," how can we show our salvation in an economically troubled world? By what financial service to the poor? With what biblical sense of justice?

91

The earth is the LORD's and all that is in it, the world,
and those who live in it.

PSALM 24:1

Many of us who read this meditation rank among the world's materially wealthy people. We are the economically privileged. In North America, even those of us with modest incomes have vastly more financial power than the bulk of the world's population.

True, we may not *feel* terribly rich. But that's only because we have lost our perspective. When yesterday's luxuries become today's necessities, when we keep comparing ourselves with people even wealthier than ourselves, when out of custom we "talk poor" and restrict our cash flow with immediate reinvestment, then we can fool ourselves into thinking we are not so very well off. News magazines report that a fair number of people whose annual income ranks in the top five percent feel uncomfortably pinched — a fact that brings tears to the eyes of the rest of the population.

Let's face the truth. By world standards most of us are prosperous. Let's face another truth. We are therefore "the rich" whom the Bible addresses so pointedly and with such fearful warnings. Let's face a third truth. None of our wealth is ours. The earth is the Lord's. The

Questions about Our Salvation

fullness of our granaries is the Lord's. So is our gross national product. Our "personal assets" are not personally ours.

Salvation is a free gift of God. Wealth is not. It comes with strings attached. It's given only in trust. We are all trustees. We've been entrusted with varying amounts of the Lord's vast resources. One day we will need to account for what we have done with those resources. It's likely to be embarrassing or worse. Even now, if all bank-card statements were open and all checkbook entries known, our poverty-stricken brothers and sisters would be dismayed.

The question for trustees is never the question that first comes to our mind. Our question is not, "All right, how much do I have to give away?" That question still assumes we own our wealth. The real question is far more troubling: in the face of God and the world's poor, *how much do I dare keep for myself?*

227

> *O Lord our God, help us to look at ourselves without evasion. Then help us to look at those who have far less than we. Finally help us understand that you care deeply what we do next. Through Jesus Christ, Amen.*

How Should We Handle Our Wealth?

92

> *But fornication and impurity of any kind, or greed,*
> *must not even be mentioned among you, as is proper*
> *among saints.*
>
> EPHESIANS 5:3

Years ago, conservative Christians asked each other a test question about theater attendance. "Suppose Jesus returned," they said. "Would you want him to find you in a theater?"

Make the question more contemporary. "What if he returned while you watching a porn site's 'live show'? Wouldn't you be ashamed?"

But suppose he found us not at a porn show, but at a fashion show. Suppose he found us lusting after designer jeans or the latest fashion in evening gowns. Suppose he found us in an atmosphere of materialism, greed, and snobbery. Is this a better theater? Are these more godly lusts? Even though the clothes are on instead of off, is the whole show much less obscene?

The Bible is against unchastity — what it calls *porneia* (por-NAY-ah). It is also against greed — what it calls *pleonexia* (pleh-oh-NEX-ee-ah). The Bible is against them in the same breath and the same text. Both are unthinkable for Christians. Both show an unseemly itch, an almost unmentionable human weakness.

Questions about Our Salvation

Pleonexia is the "annexing of more." If I have a DVD player, and 80 DVD's, but keep hankering for more, insatiably for more and more — and then for still more — I'm a moral clown as a Christian. I display the "more" syndrome. The same is true for land, cash, jewelry, and motorized toys for grown-ups.

The problem is that our society thinks *pleonexia* is just fine. Products trigger it. Advertising assumes it. Our whole economy depends on it. *Pleonexia* helps to keep the market moving. This makes financial obedience to the Lord considerably harder for all of us.

But we have to keep trying. Teaching our children to laugh at television commercials, boycotting planned obsolescence, rejoicing to see how many wonderful goods we can do without, we have to fight back in an acquisitive society.

And one day the Lord who came to set at liberty those who are oppressed may set *us* free — free from the lust for more.

> *O Lord, liberate us from the lust for more. Let us rejoice in small occasions and simple things. Through Jesus Christ our Lord, Amen.*

How Should We Handle Our Wealth?

93

How does God's love abide in anyone who has the world's goods and sees a brother or sister in need and yet refuses help?

1 JOHN 3:17

We are the rich. We *do* have "the world's goods." We are trying hard not to want even more of those goods.

But do we see our "brother or sister in need"? We do. Television news programs have shown us the world's famines. We have seen skinny mothers holding their spindly infants. We have seen the little kids with their sad faces — kids with legs you could circle with thumb and forefinger. Even in rich countries like the United States and Canada, some household pets eat better than some people. Homeless children move from one welfare hotel to another, never secure, never properly fed and housed. In large cities, homeless adults shop in restaurant garbage bins. We see them.

And yet, in another way, we do not. We don't *really* see them — not with enough compassion and indignation to do something about it. We don't want to see human need that way. It's unpleasant. And perhaps we're secretly afraid that too much indignation over financial inequality might develop into full-fledged economic reform. Reluc-

Questions about Our Salvation

tantly, but deliberately, we "refuse help" for the poor. Like Lazarus at the rich man's door, the poor become merely a part of the landscape. They may have all the crumbs they like, just so they make themselves scarce.

How do we refuse help? Few of us have the heart to say that the poor *deserve* their misery — that the reason for the awkward difference between them and us is that they are bad and we are good, that they are degenerate while we are upright. We don't dare say any of that because we know that's not what the Bible teaches. The Bible warns the rich and seeks to protect the poor.

No, we refuse help in other ways. We *all* do. We say the problem of poverty is too big, too remote, too complex, too disturbing. Besides, none of our close friends is poor. And so we go on, feeling guilty at times, but essentially unchanged.

"How does God's love abide in anyone who has the world's goods and sees a brother or sister in need and yet refuses help?"

> O LORD, *do not rebuke me in your anger, or discipline me in your wrath. It is for you, O LORD, that I wait. Do not forsake me, O LORD; do not be far from me. Make haste to help me, O Lord, my salvation. Amen.*
>
> — FROM PSALM 38

How Should We Handle Our Wealth?

94

Those who oppress the poor insult their Maker, but those who are kind to the needy honor him.

PROVERBS 14:31

Whoever is kind to the poor lends to the LORD.

PROVERBS 19:17

The entire Bible tells us that God cares for the poor in a special way. The poor have God's ear, God's concern, God on their side. God's care for the poor is so intense, his identification with them so strong, that any of us who oppresses the poor insults not only them, but also God himself! "Those who oppress the poor insult their *maker.*"

Thus we are called not only to see the poor but also to take responsibility for them. We may not let them struggle on their own. We may not provoke them by flaunting fancy possessions. As Isaiah 32 says, we may not "ruin the poor with lying words" by making those ruinous generalizations we've all heard. "They're too dumb to learn. They're too lazy to work. They're too ignorant to vote." Instead, those who are "kind to the needy" defend them. And, as Ernest Campbell somewhere says, in their politics people who are kind to the needy

Questions about Our Salvation

fight "the mood that would see more done for those who have enough already and less for those who lack."

Biblically faithful Christians take a stand with those who "have not." For, once again, God watches personally how we act in this. "God sends us the poor as *his* receivers," says the reformer John Calvin. "Whoever is kind to the poor lends to the Lord," says the Bible.

The Bible doesn't talk first about charity for the poor. It doesn't assume that we ought to keep all the power. There is no biblical warrant for patronizing poor people.

Rather, the Bible talks first about justice, about the rights of the poor, about the fact that the poor have a moral claim on us. "The righteous know the rights of the poor; the wicked have no such understanding" (Prov. 29:7).

Talk about justice, rights, and claims is the hardest talk of all. That is, after all, the kind of talk that touches off revolution — or, if we act before it's too late, godly economic reform.

233

> *O Lord, give justice to the weak and the orphan; maintain the right of the lowly and the destitute. Rescue the weak and the needy; deliver them from the hand of the wicked. In Jesus' name, Amen.*
>
> — FROM PSALM 82

How Should We Handle Our Wealth?

95

For, as I can testify, they voluntarily gave according to their means, and even beyond their means, begging us earnestly for the privilege of sharing in this ministry to the saints.

2 CORINTHIANS 8:3-4

In a prophetic book about prosperity in the midst of poverty, *Rich Christians in an Age of Hunger,* Ronald Sider suggests that we who are upwardly mobile ought to keep on increasing not only the amount but also the percentage of our income that we give away. Thus, if a Christian now gives 10 percent, perhaps later he or she could give 20 percent or 30 percent or 50 percent. What Sider opposes is the simple assumption — widespread even in the Christian church — that our standard of living ought to increase automatically and proportionately with our income. Not necessarily. If even the government taxes on a graduated scale, can the Christian church be content with a lesser righteousness? Why not a "graduated tithe"?

Certain Christians have already begun. These are *heroes of giving* — people who, though rich, become poorer so that others might become richer. Like the Macedonians whom Paul praises in the Scripture passage, these Christians count it a privilege to give according to

Questions about Our Salvation

their means, and even beyond them. Here are people who, though having the form of prosperity, do not count keeping up with the Joneses a thing to be grasped, but empty themselves and take on the form of servants.

How do they dare? How do they dare reduce their own comfort level and endanger their own financial security? Where did they ever get this idea of self-sacrifice?

They got it from Jesus Christ. And they dare to do it because they have no fear. We are often *afraid* to give because we are privately banking on financial security as our main comfort in life and death. Thus, instead of celebrating the opportunity to give, we shrink back and build bigger barns for our goods.

But we know it won't work. Our wealth won't last. In a terrorized world, none of our earthly securities is really secure. And someday all our earthly goods will be either a reproach to us or a sheer irrelevance. For what we "take with us" when we die is only so much as we have given away.

> *Merciful God, we remember our Lord Jesus Christ who,*
> *though rich, became poor for our sakes so that we, in*
> *our poverty, might become rich. Amen.*

How Should We Handle Our Wealth?

How Can the Forgiven Forgive?

The Bible connects our duties as saved people with the acts of God and Christ. The small word "as" often serves as the link. "Love one another as I have loved you" (John 15:12). "Just as the Lord has forgiven you, so you also must forgive" (Col. 3:13). "Be kind to one another, tenderhearted, forgiving one another, as God in Christ has forgiven you" (Eph. 4:32).

Robert Roberts says that forgiveness means letting go of anger that we have a right to. To do this takes a lot of spiritual muscle, and the job is almost impossible for people who themselves feel unforgiven. But forgiveness is the soul of our life together. We are forgiven to forgive.

But how can we do it?

96

*I said, "I will confess my transgressions to the LORD,"
and you forgave the guilt of my sin. Be glad in the LORD
and rejoice, O righteous, and shout for joy, all you upright in heart.*

PSALM 32:5, 11

For many contemporary people, life has lost all religious dimension. These people live a flat life, recognizing neither the depths of their sin nor the heights of God's grace. Perhaps they do get high on a number of stiff drinks. Perhaps they are indeed laid low the next morning. But for them life mostly stretches out in a plain.

The two main dimensions of human life since the Fall are sin and grace. We can't live with God, with each other, or even with ourselves until we see how great is our sin and how much greater is God's grace. When the Christian life goes flat, look for some loss of sensitivity to sin or grace.

The loss shows up all over the place. In church we confess our sin and receive an assurance of pardon, but neither means very much to us. Some churches have simply dropped this part of the service. David H. C. Read once remarked that confession and pardon easily become trivial to us. If you can't quite catch a person's words, you say, "I beg

Questions about Our Salvation

your pardon." It's merely a way of saying, "Speak up, please!" If you get a wrong telephone number, you say, "I'm sorry." The other person says, "Forget it." And you both do. It's a small thing. Life goes on.

Sometimes that's the way we feel about sin and forgiveness. It's often just a ritual. "I beg your pardon," we say to God. "Forget it," we think God says. "It's no big deal."

Here is trivial Christianity for trivial people — for people who fall asleep in church, drift through prayers, and flatten the Christian faith out to a tasteless little slice of life.

The Bible shows us a more excellent way, full of heights and depths. Prayers from the depths whisper guilt and yearn for pardon. Prayers from the heights shout praise to God for mighty acts of mercy.

The movement from one prayer to the other has come through forgiveness.

> *Have mercy on me, O God, according to your steadfast love; according to your abundant mercy blot out my transgressions. Create in me a clean heart, O God, and put a new and right spirit within me. Restore to me the joy of your salvation, and sustain in me a willing spirit. Through Jesus Christ, Amen.*
>
> — FROM PSALM 51

How Can the Forgiven Forgive?

97

You wicked slave! I forgave you all that debt because
you pleaded with me. Should you not have had mercy
on your fellow slave, as I had mercy on you?

MATTHEW 18:32-33

Serious Christians take sin seriously. Any of us who has been attacked or ignored knows that sin is no joke. We don't say, "It doesn't matter." It does. Sin hurts.

But shouldn't real Christians be more tolerant? Not at all. The Bible never tells us to tolerate sin or to condone it. The Bible tells us to *forgive* sin. Tolerance overlooks sin; forgiveness absorbs sin and then finds ways to soften its heart toward the sinner.

The grace of God to forgiven people can overflow in wonderful ways. When it does, grace abounds, and especially in the form of forgiveness. How perfectly fitting for those who have been forgiven to keep the momentum going by forgiving others! How Christ-like to absorb evil without passing it on! And how necessary for health in the body of Christ. We can't have health without reconciliation, and we can't have reconciliation without forgiveness. In fact, being reconciled with others is so central to the life of the Christian community that we can't even worship God until we have taken steps to be reconciled to a

Questions about Our Salvation

person with whom we are at odds (Matt. 5:23-24). The church is a body of people who know they have been unbelievably pardoned — and who *therefore* turn toward each other with unusually generous forgiveness.

The communion of saints is impossible without the forgiveness of sins.

Jesus tells the parable of a man who has just been forgiven a debt of twenty million dollars. As soon as his debt is forgiven, the man turns around to collect forty dollars from another servant. One moment he's on his knees, begging his master, "Lord, have patience with me"; the next moment, released and forgiven, he's back on his feet, squeezing some fellow servant and demanding, "Pay up!"

Helmut Thielicke once remarked that God forgives us an accumulated debt so great that it buckled the knees of God's Son. And yet we steam and fret, toss and turn, over even the smallest — over even *imagined* — snubs by a brother or sister.

How is this possible?

> *Gracious God, impress us so deeply with the knowledge of your grace that we turn in grace to brothers and sisters. Let your grace abound, O God. Through Jesus Christ our Lord, Amen.*

How Can the Forgiven Forgive?

98

Then Peter came to Jesus and asked, "Lord, how many times shall I forgive my brother when he sins against me? Up to seven times?" Jesus answered, "I tell you, not seven times, but seventy-seven times."

MATTHEW 18:21-22

So if you have been raised with Christ . . . forgive each other.

COLOSSIANS 3:1, 13

It's hard to repent. And while it's hard enough to repent before a perfect God, it's even harder to repent before an imperfect human being. To admit that you have injured or neglected another person, then to go to the person and say, "I'm sorry. I'm ashamed. Will you forgive me?" — to do this is *mortifying*. It kills us to do it. You need to be a big person even to give it a serious try. That's the paradox of repentance, says C. S. Lewis. Only a bad person needs to repent. Only a good person can do it.

If it's hard to repent, it's just as hard to forgive. I spoke in the last meditation about God's grace flowing all around a Christian commu-

Questions about Our Salvation

nity as good people forgive each other. Amazing grace, how sweet the sound!

But, of course, we know how tough it is to forgive somebody who has really hurt us. Suppose someone tells a lie that gets you fired. Suppose someone humiliates a defenseless member of your family. Suppose someone violates your child!

Forgive? You feel as if you want to kill! Forgive this? As Lewis says, the call to forgiveness can sound like too low a calling. It can sound contemptible. Forgive *this?* As if it didn't matter?

Of course it matters. Sometimes an offender hurts us to the core. Some hurts go so deep that we may not be able to forgive for a time, and maybe not for a long time. Some hurts are harder to forgive than others. Some offenses spring to mind years after we thought we'd dropped them, and we have to forgive them all over again. Maybe seventy-seven times.

"Forgiveness is a journey," writes Lewis Smedes. "The deeper the offense, the longer the journey."

Why is it so hard to forgive? Because to give up justified anger is mortifying. It kills us to do it. In this way repentance and forgiveness are a natural pair. Each is a kind of death. Both can bring new life. They are ways of dying and rising with Jesus Christ.

> *O God, let Christ dwell in our hearts through faith, so that we may know the love of Christ that surpasses knowledge, and be filled with your own fullness. Amen.*
>
> — FROM EPHESIANS 3

How Can the Forgiven Forgive?

99

And forgive us our debts, as we also have forgiven our debtors.

MATTHEW 6:12

In this famous petition of our Lord's Prayer, we ask forgiveness while simultaneously declaring our debtors forgiven. We pray, "Forgive us, O God, just as we have right now declared others forgiven." "Cancel our debt as we have, at this moment, cancelled our neighbor's debt."

The idea is that we can't ask forgiveness of God while refusing it for others. Every time we pray this prayer, we declare our neighbors forgiven. Of course, we may not *feel* terribly forgiving toward them. We may not even like them. That's not the point. Forgiveness is not a feeling but an act. It's something you *do.*

What do you do, exactly, when you forgive? Jay Adams and other Christian thinkers have suggested several considerations.

First, if I forgive a person, I promise not to let his offense "come between us" anymore. I no longer hold my anger against him; I let it drop. I ought to be able to look him in the eye and speak with him. Perhaps this is one person I can't laugh with, at least not for a time and maybe never. And perhaps I can't forget what was done. But it's just that — it's *done* now. I put the offense in the past and keep it there.

Questions about Our Salvation

Second, I promise not to use this incident against this person in the future. I will not bring it up in public or explore it with friends. And, if I bury the hatchet with this person, I will not later go back and dig it up.

Finally, if I cancel someone's sin, I quit nursing my memory of it. Lewis Smedes reminds us that nursing a grievance provides a delicious pain — like a tongue that keeps going to a sore place in our mouth. But to forgive is to exercise mind control and to declare an old injury off limits for private thoughts.

Three steps in forgiveness. They are hard steps. But we have our Lord's footprints to follow. We forgive, simply put, in order to die and rise with Jesus Christ — not only in our baptism, but also in our relationships. Three hard steps, but they lead to peace. And even a good night's sleep.

Our Father in heaven, forgive us our debts as we have now forgiven our debtors. For yours is the kingdom and the power and the glory forever. Amen.

How Can the Forgiven Forgive?

100

*But Esau said, "I have enough, my brother. . . ." Jacob
said, "No, please; if I find favor with you, then accept
my present from my hand; for truly to see your face is
like seeing the face of God — since you have received
me with such favor."*

GENESIS 33:9-10

In *The Forgiving Community,* William Klaassen reports a question Abigail Van Buren ("Dear Abby") once asked her readers. Abby asked, "Is there a reader somewhere who has caught her husband being unfaithful, has forgiven him, and has since had a happy marriage?"

The response was heavy. Many people who answered said that the knowledge of adultery caused a particularly acute suffering. They had reacted with anger, shame, and a sense of great insecurity. Their spouse's infidelity upset them more than they could say. But, interestingly, a number of the respondents also testified to the power of forgiveness. They knew the scars would remain, but for those who were determined to go on, the forgiveness that they were able to offer had helped them and their marriages grow stronger.

Forgiveness has great power. It opens the channels of grace in the Christian community, in a marriage, among friends, between parent

Questions about Our Salvation

and child. While forgiveness must be Christlike in the pain it suffers, it is also Christlike in its steady determination to deal again with the offending person. Together, repentance and forgiveness liberate people.

And one of the strangest and most wonderful discoveries we make when we forgive is that forgiveness can do more than just restore a broken relationship; it can actually strengthen it. People who meet each other halfway, one seeking forgiveness and the other seeking to grant it, often find that their love for each other has deepened. Not always. But, in God's grace, sometimes.

Jacob goes limping into a sunrise on his way to meet the brother he had so cunningly cheated. Jacob has learned humility by wrestling with God. Esau, in turn, is able to call Jacob "my brother." Across all the years they come together in a reconciliation that has the grace of heaven all over it. Once Jacob had as much as called his brother a fool. But not on reconciliation day: "Truly to see your face is like seeing the face of God, since you have received me with such favor."

O God, may all who seek you rejoice and be glad in you; may those who love your salvation tell of your great mercy. In Jesus' name, Amen.
— FROM PSALM 40

How Can the Forgiven Forgive?

Question 21

What Is the Shape
of the Godly Life?

People have various recipes for "the good life." Playboys, for example, serve two masters: lust and greed. Macho folks promote a saving trio of G's: God, guns, and guts.

Christians promote godliness. We describe the godly life with many phrases. We call it "life in Christ," or "the new life," or "covenant life," or "the transformed life." Because obedience to the will of God is so central in Godly living, we call it "the obedient life." Or, we call it simply "the Christian life."

A rich young man asked Jesus, "What shall I do to be saved?" We ask, "What shall we do now that we are saved?" What is the shape of the Godly life?

101

Go into your room and shut the door and pray.

MATTHEW 6:6

[Be] nourished on the words of the faith.

1 TIMOTHY 4:6

Come, let us worship and bow down.

PSALM 95:6

Sing to the LORD, *bless his name.*

PSALM 96:2

*Whatever is pure, whatever is pleasing . . . think about
these things.*

PHILIPPIANS 4:8

*Examine yourselves, and only then eat of the bread and
drink of the cup.*

1 CORINTHIANS 11:28

Questions about Our Salvation

Godliness is the proper manner of life before God. It includes believing right doctrine; rejecting myths and believing the truth is a *Godly* thing to do. It includes social action; to liberate the oppressed is a *Godly* thing to do. And it includes devotional piety — the whole range of religious acts described in the Scripture passages above; praying, reading the Bible, worshiping, praising, meditating, and celebrating the Lord's Supper — all these are Godly things to do.

Some of these devotional acts we perform with others. We worship publicly. We sing together. We celebrate communion. But much devotional piety is private. Each of us needs time — regular time — when we go into a room, shut the door, and do our exercises. This is a time for confessing personal sin, giving thanks for a particular mercy, asking for the measure of God's grace we need. This is a time for gauging the drift of our lives and for making a moral resolve. This is a time for reading the Bible, for exploring its deep places and taking to heart its counsel.

Personal devotions often stir in us a powerful sense of God's presence. We may sense some of the beauty of God that we can't describe to others very well, and maybe don't wish to.

But those feelings are special graces, secret reassurances. We won't always feel them. Still we keep on. That's because devotions are not so much something we feel as something we do. We exercise faith. We *train* ourselves in godliness (1 Tim. 4:7).

Spiritual exercise is like jogging. You often do it gladly. But you are no hypocrite if you jog even when you don't feel like it.

> *O God, you are my God, I seek you, my soul thirsts for you; my flesh faints for you. Because your steadfast love is better than life, my lips will praise you. Through Jesus Christ, Amen.*
> — FROM PSALM 63

What Is the Shape of the Godly Life?

102

Jesus said to him, "You shall love the Lord your God with all your heart, and with all your soul, and with all your mind."

MATTHEW 22:37

Karl Barth, one of the most learned and productive of twentieth-century theologians, had a richly furnished mind and a fertile theological imagination. He wrote volumes and volumes of theology, much of it technical, refined, sophisticated. Even Christians who think Barth was wrong often think that he was *interestingly* wrong.

According to one version of a famous story, Barth was once asked about his vast theological accomplishment. What was its center? "If you had to sum up all your work," someone asked, "what would you say?"

Barth's reply was disarming: "Jesus loves me. This I know — for the Bible tells me so."

Here, as Barth rightly believed, is a place to stand. And a place to start. Perhaps it's even a place to end our study of the words and truths of the faith. But meanwhile mature Christians will have explored far and wide in their attempts to love God with all their mind. They will want to know as much of the faith as they can. They will want as much

Questions about Our Salvation

as they can get of what Paul calls "sound doctrine." They want to say "Jesus loves me" as a *summary,* not a slogan.

"You shall love the Lord your God with all your heart, and with all your soul, and with all your mind," says our Lord. In other words, you shall love God with everything you have and everything you are. Everything. Every longing, every endowment, each of your intellectual gifts, any athletic talent or computer skill, all capacity for delight, every good thing that has your fingerprints on it — take all this, says Jesus, and refer it to God. Take your longing, and long for God; take your creaturely riches, and endow God; take your eye for beauty, and appreciate God. With your heart and soul and mind, with all your needs and splendors, make a full turn toward God.

To become more Godly is to become a better lover. Becoming a better lover of God means taking an interest in God, learning some of the life of God, discovering the purposes of God. It means giving God the benefit of the doubt when injustice or suffering make God look bad.

Loving God with all our mind means that we will think hard about our faith, and then be willing to take the hit if someone accuses us of theology.

> *Make me to know your ways, O Lord; teach me your paths. Lead me in your truth, and teach me, through Jesus Christ our Lord. Amen.*
> — FROM PSALM 25

What Is the Shape of the Godly Life?

103

*You shall love the Lord your God with all your heart,
and with all your soul, and with all your mind. . . . You
shall love your neighbor as yourself.*

MATTHEW 22:37-39

Parents who let their child visit someone else's house for a day often do it uneasily. What if he hogs all the toys? What if at lunch she prays one of those unusual prayers again? What if he tells lies about our family? Worse, what if he tells the truth?

Before you leave, you plead with your child. "Please," you say, "try to be good."

Try to be good. No doubt it's a high calling. But the Bible talks much less about being good than about *doing* good. And though worldly people sometimes wish Christians would do their good somewhere else, biblically instructed people think of doing good as a main delight of the new life.

What kind of good? All kinds. Every kind. In as many areas of life as sin has done bad — in that many areas Christians do good. The right strategy is to fit our own work into Jesus Christ's great work of restoring a corrupted creation.

We all know how human beings can corrupt a good thing. Some-

Questions about Our Salvation

one has observed that for centuries "Bethlehem" has been a favorite name among Christians for hospitals. It seems right to associate these places of mercy with the birth of our Lord. One hospital, in particular, was in London. Over the years, the hospital's name was shortened and slurred from Bethlehem to "Bedlam." People called "lunatics" and "maniacs" were kept there. Eventually the hospital began to charge admittance for those who wanted to come in to gawk at the patients.

Sinners turn Bethlehem to Bedlam. Redeemed sinners try to turn it back. A cheerful Christian nursing-home attendant cleans up after helpless human beings. A keen businessperson attempts to create jobs for jobless people. A forest manager goes daily about the wonderful task of preserving and restoring a part of God's creation. In thousands of ingenious ways, the followers of Jesus Christ seek to show their love for God and neighbor by turning sickness to health, depression to hope, ignorance to knowledge, Bedlam to Bethlehem.

O God, let us be steadfast, immovable, abounding in the work of Jesus Christ, always aware that, in him, our labor is not in vain. Amen.

— FROM 1 CORINTHIANS 15:58

What Is the Shape of the Godly Life?

104

While he was at Bethany . . . a woman came with an alabaster jar of very costly ointment of nard, and she broke open the jar and poured the ointment on his head. . . . And they scolded her. But Jesus said, "Let her alone. She has performed a good service for me. . . . She has done what she could."

MARK 14:3-8

The Godly life is shaped by the law of love for God and neighbor. And love means doing good.

But do we all have to do the same thing? Do we all have to do the *same* good?

Christians used to glare at each other over discussions of whether individual witnessing or social action was more necessary. We now know both are required. Do you try for individual conversions or for changed social structures? Both. Do you testify to your next-door neighbor or to a government bureaucracy? Both.

But who is equal to all these things? Who has sufficient time and talent for them? Nobody — at least not "personally." Of course, we can verbally encourage Christians who are doing work different from ours, and we should. We can pray for other sorts of work, and we do.

Questions about Our Salvation

We can send a check (which represents our work) to support still other kinds of good work, and we will. But none of us can do everything. None of us can do social work in Appalachia, inner-city ministry in the South Bronx, hospital counseling downtown, neighborhood Bible study on our own block — all the while preparing a new Chinese translation of the Bible and caring for our own children.

We get into trouble in the Christian community when we start issuing identical marching orders for all Christians, as if each of us must follow Christ in exactly the same way.

Jesus himself cuts through all that. A woman has ministered to him in a lavish and peculiar way. She has drenched him with perfume. With a whiplash in his voice, Jesus says to the disgusted bystanders, "Let her alone. She has performed a good service for me. She has done what she could."

She has contributed in her own style. She has done a unique sort of thing. She has done what she could.

Thank you, O God, for the good gifts and works of your sons and daughters all over the world. Thank you for their faith, for their understanding, and for their works of love. Through Jesus Christ our Lord, Amen.

What Is the Shape of the Godly Life?

105

So let us not grow weary in doing what is right, for we will reap at harvest-time, if we do not give up.

GALATIANS 6:9

It's the first good day of spring. Someone asks you to wash the car. At first you don't relish the idea, but gradually you get into the spirit of car washing. You not only wash that car thoroughly and dry it with a chamois to prevent water spots; you also vacuum it out, take some cleaner to the bug spots and tar splashes, and start in on a bit of waxing and polishing.

It hasn't been so bad, actually. You get into a job and pretty soon you see yourself as a person to watch, a trendsetter in personal industry. You see yourself moving to bigger and better tasks. When the car is done, then you'll clean out the garage and put up the awnings. After that you'll rake, mow, and edge the lawn. Next you'll move over to your neighbor's lawn and then clean his basement — on and on as you demonstrate to yourself, to your family, to the whole neighborhood what a real worker can do.

Then, as you wax and whistle, your back starts to ache and your right arm begins to feel heavy and sore. Your whistling slides down into a slower rhythm and shifts into a minor key.

Questions about Our Salvation

Drop by drop your enthusiasm begins to dribble away. Perhaps you'd better leave the basement for another day. And the lawn too, you guess. And the garage can wait. Doing this car is a big enough job all by itself. Well, leave the rest of the car for next Saturday too. Now find a hammock!

"Let us not grow weary in doing what is right." At some time or another most of us have felt a sense of adventure in the Christian life; we have also felt a pain in the neck and all the adventure running off in sweat. We have known not only the rush of enthusiasm for doing good in the name of Christ but also that sinking sense of futility when others don't notice or care.

"We will reap at harvest-time," says St. Paul, "if we do not give up." Here is a word for any of us who have been Christian do-gooders until we can't move another muscle or think another thought or make one more telephone call. For all spent-out Christians a heartening word: we will reap the fruit of the Spirit in a life which never ends.

If we do not give up.

> *O God, I am continually with you. You hold my right hand. My flesh and my heart may fail, but you are the strength of my heart and my portion forever. In Jesus' name, Amen.*
>
> — FROM PSALM 73

What Is the Shape of the Godly Life?

Questions about the Church

Question 22

What Is the Nature
of the Church?

None of us is saved alone. We are redeemed and then commissioned for God's mission in the world as part of a people, members of a body, participants in a living community.

The church is a community gathered by Christ and empowered to be his witnesses, agents, and models in the world. Unbelievers sometimes look at the church with "a scornful wonder," as one of the old hymns says. But even Christians can get impatient and frustrated with how life goes in the Christian church.

So let's ask some questions about the church, beginning with a basic one: What, exactly, is the church? A person who recites the Apostles' Creed says, "I believe a holy catholic church, the communion of saints." But what does that mean?

106

[Make] every effort to maintain the unity of the Spirit in the bond of peace. There is one body and one Spirit, just as you were called to the one hope of your calling, one Lord, one faith, one baptism, one God and Father of all, who is above all and through all and in all.

EPHESIANS 4:3-6

Variety is often a treasure. An old-fashioned garden presents a splendid variety of grasses, ferns, and flowers. A well-stocked fish market features a wide variety of dried, fresh, and frozen seafood. A Saturday farmer's market offers fresh fruits and vegetables in a wonderful array of sizes, shapes, and colors. All this is a sign of God's goodness, said John Calvin. We could have gotten along with just a few kinds of foods and flowers. But God wants to delight us. So God's love and imagination have gone to work and now we have fruits as different from each other as a banana and a plum.

Yet God made only one church. Christians believe there is *one* holy catholic church." Here it is we, and not God, who have introduced variety. I don't mean that God has no hand in the colorful spectrum of music, clothing, language, gesture, and other cultural adaptations of the gospel. These are as delightful as bananas and plums. I mean that God is not the one who has splintered the church into pieces that are indifferent or hostile to one another. One God has called one people to be one body. It is we who have divided the body.

Questions about the Church

The divisions keep on across the centuries, across the world. North America by itself has hundreds of varieties of churches. A yearbook of churches lists not only usual churches — Greek Orthodox, Catholic, Lutheran, Presbyterian, Baptist, Methodist — but also some less usual ones — Kodesh Church of Immanuel, Fire Baptized Holiness Church, Church of the Foursquare Gospel of Western Canada, Church of Daniel's Band, Christian Reformed Church. And, more recently, churches that aren't called churches at all, but "assemblies," "ministries," "worship centers," "communities for spiritual formation."

Some of the variety is just fine. Local churches, for example, can organize for particular missions in the world. But some of the variety is owed to sinful division. Christians are supposed to be one body, *visibly*. But we are not. And our divisions are a scandal before the face of heaven and earth. *Schism*, the breach of union in the church, is a tragedy, like divorce. It's a painful tearing, like pulling a limb from a body. Doctrine, communion, ordination of women, views of homosexuality, even whether to sing one hymn and two praise songs, or the other way around — all these and many more issues have become blades that cut the membrane of unity.

But what can we do? Declare ourselves alone to be right and invite all others to be converted to us? Or say it really doesn't matter what the various churches practice and believe, and the more diversity, the better? Or give up our own confession and practice just because other Christians reject it?

No, three times. But, again, what can we do about the splintering of the church?

Could we, perhaps, begin by trying to keep the unity of the Spirit in the local church to which we now belong?

> *Forgive us, O God, for grieving you with our divisions.*
> *Forgive our church sin. Forgive, correct, and heal us by*
> *your Spirit. Amen.*

What Is the Nature of the Church?

107

"Moses did not know that the skin of his face shone be-cause he had been talking with God."

EXODUS 34:29

You are . . . a holy nation in order that you may pro-claim the mighty acts of him who called you out of darkness and into his glorious light.

1 PETER 2:9

At its cynical worst, contemporary society sees "saints" as either hypo-crites (nobody is *that* good) or else as airheads. Saints are impostors who deserve to be unmasked, or else they are childish dreamers who waste their lives chasing lost causes.

The fact is that all Christians are called to be saints. We are called not to be hypocrites or dreamers, but to live "set-apart" lives that wit-ness to the mighty acts of God. A saint is a person, said C. S. Lewis, "who makes God believable." A saint is a person who brings God to us in the way she speaks and listens, in the way she stands strong for jus-tice, in the way she weeps with those who weep. A saint is willing to be inconvenienced, even persecuted, for the sake of the gospel, but she

Questions about the Church

doesn't think so much about how hard the gospel is. She thinks of its urgency and beauty. When Moses came down the mountain after speaking with God, his face shone. But he didn't know it because he was thinking of God, not looking in a mirror.

The Old Testament people of God were set apart to be a blessing to the nations. The church of Jesus Christ has been set apart to pursue the same mission. Sainthood isn't for sitting around and adjusting our haloes. Sainthood is for serving the world in the name of Jesus Christ.

And so often we'd like to pass. Sainthood is far beyond our modest wishes. We are like a man whose doctor tells him that the best thing for him is to quit smoking. "I don't deserve the best, Doc," says the man. "What's second best?"

The holy catholic church is too often satisfied with second best. On our liberal side we learn to cuss a little, to smile at simple piety, and to reassure skeptics that miracles aren't as miraculous as they used to be. On our conservative side we hustle the Christian religion with celebrities, television freebies, and nightclub formats for worship. We don't try to be so holy. And the world watches us succeed.

The trouble with such worldliness is that it takes the shine off our faces. Nobody can see any of "the glorious light." And then God is no longer as believable as he was before.

O Lord, let there be light. Let your light shine. Let it shine, through Jesus Christ our Lord. Amen.

What Is the Nature of the Church?

108

*[God] has put all things under [Christ's] feet and has
made him the head over all things for the church, which
is his body, the fullness of him who fills all in all.*

EPHESIANS 1:22-23

In *The Significance of the Church*, Raymond McAfee Brown says that it
would be just fine to call oneself a "Protestant Catholic." If we believe
in the lordship of Jesus Christ over the whole church, we are catholic
Christians. We believe a *catholic* church — that is, a universal church.
We may not be a *Roman* catholic, but we are still catholic.

The church across the world and across time is a lot bigger than
our vision of it. Sometimes we let our vision of the church shrink so
small that it includes only our own little denomination in our own
country — or, worse, only our own local or independent church in
our own city or town. *That* is "the church" to us. And, clinging to such
a shrunken idea of the church, we sometimes feel more at home with
native secularists than with foreign Christians.

This is a mistake. When we celebrate the Lord's Supper, we should
think with awe and warmth of the millions of Christians across the
world and across history who say with us: "The body of Christ given
for you"; "The blood of Christ shed for you." When we see African

Questions about the Church

Christians feeding starving people where every government agency has failed, we should feel their triumph. When we read of Iraqi Christians being squeezed by our nation's state department, we should feel their pain. Our nation is hurting our church. When one member of the church suffers, all suffer. This is part of being a Protestant catholic.

A certain modern confession says, "Each member is the church in the world." That's not quite right. You are not the church in the world; I am not the church. Instead, we are individually *members* of the universal church in the world — a church so vast, so deep, so old, so multinational, so incredibly catholic that only the Lord of the universe can be its head.

> *O God, your power raised Jesus Christ from the dead, and seated him at your right hand in the heavenly places, putting all things under his feet, making him head over all things for the church. Glory to you, O God, through Jesus Christ, Amen.*

What Is the Nature of the Church?

109

Now you are the body of Christ.

1 CORINTHIANS 12:27

You are . . . God's own people.

1 PETER 2:9

To all God's beloved in Rome, who are called to be saints.

ROMANS 1:7

We sometimes hear people discussing a certain local church as if it were someone's local business. Just as people refer to "Ed's Breads" or to "Janie's Cookies," they refer to a church by the name of its minister. Thus a church in which the Reverend Allis Chalmers is senior pastor gets to be known as "Chalmers's Church."

There may be good reason for the name. Perhaps Mr. Chalmers thinks of himself less as the congregation's servant than as its boss. Perhaps he "runs" the church, conforming it to his plans, steering it in

Questions about the Church

the direction of his goals, impressing on it his personality and style. He is the captain. The church is the ship. "Chalmers's Church."

The New Testament takes another view. Many of its descriptions of the church impress us with the fact that it belongs to no human being. The original catholic church in Rome is not "Paul's church." It's not even St. Peter's. It's "God's beloved."

The body of Christ, the temple of God, the bride of Christ, the people of God — these wonderful phrases tell us that the church is all about belonging. Even the word *church* reflects this fact. The English word *church* (like the German *Kirche*) is derived from a Greek word that means "belonging to the Lord." The church belongs to the Lord of the church.

What follows from this? A great deal. The institutional church is not our club to be rigged up to suit ourselves and to meet our own religious needs. The church is rather a living instrument of Jesus Christ, equipped to do his work in the world. It is set up to serve not only ourselves but also those outside our gathering. We do not form ourselves into a church by our voluntary cooperation. We are rather *called* as a people to praise God, to serve his children, and to give ourselves for others in the same way as Christ sacrificed himself for us. In other words, the Christian church is an agent, witness, and model of the gospel itself.

A church turned in on itself is like people who shut themselves in a closet and try to live by breathing their own carbon dioxide.

We are self-absorbed people, O God. And we live in the midst of self-absorbed people. Break us out of our tight little packs. Let us breathe the fresh air of your Spirit and serve you by serving others. Amen.

What Is the Nature of the Church?

110

They devoted themselves to the apostles' teaching and fellowship, to the breaking of bread and the prayers. All who believed were together. . . .

ACTS 2:42, 44

It's Sunday morning at the campground. A Christian family gathers around its portable television. They might have attended a local church, but the kids have persuaded the parents that it's easier to watch worship on TV. And the parents agree that the service on television is much better — bigger crowds, more dynamic "special music," real celebrities appearing instead of local wonders, and a smoother preacher with a far more fetching smile. So there the family sits, watching worship. They are a part of the wholly electronic catholic church.

Here is the church without the communion of saints. Here, as someone has said, is a "phantom, non-people church" for those who like their public worship private or who like to "go to church" without bestirring themselves or who like to change channels on a prayer that lacks pizzazz. Here is church for the convenience of those who like to discharge their weekly church obligation while munching raisin bran.

Originally, of course, the electronic church was intended to serve

Questions about the Church

shut-ins and to evangelize the unchurched. It still does both. But somehow it also tempts able-bodied church members to stay home and try to tune in a blessing. Worse, it tempts them to import electronic church formats into their own live churches so that, even there, people want to sit back passively and view religious entertainment.

This is a strange and unhappy trend. The church has always thrived on *koinonia,* on fellowship. The early Christian church experienced remarkable and revolutionary togetherness — Parthians, Medes, Elamites, Judeans, and Cappadocians together. Later on, after much struggle, racial and ethnic groups together. Weak and strong, male and female, wise old women and impatient little boys together. For centuries Christians have believed that there is no real Christian life and no real Christian faith unless it is faith and life *together.*

The church is not just a set of individuals watching television. It's a communion of living, breathing human beings, of redeemed people who worship, care, share, and serve together.

We believe "the *communion* of saints." Why not practice it?

> *Our love is short, O God, but yours is long. Our mercy is narrow, but yours is wide. Restore to us the joy of our salvation through the communion of saints. In Jesus' name, Amen.*

What Is the Nature of the Church?

Question 23

What Does the Institutional Church Do?

We can look at the Christian church in two ways. We can see it as a vast, pulsing organism — millions of professing Christians doing Christ's work in the world. Or we can see it as an organization with officers, rules, membership requirements, set services, budgets, and buildings. We call people organized in that fashion the institutional *church.*

Let's look at that institution. What is it good for? What are the "marks" of the institutional church? What does the institutional church do?

111

O come, let us worship and bow down, let us kneel before the LORD, our Maker! For he is our God.

PSALM 95:6-7

Before anything else, the Christian church worships. That is the church's main business. In response to God's mighty and gracious acts — proclaimed anew in preaching and sacraments or ordinances — the gathered church praises, thanks, and adores God. The church confesses sin, humbly asks for pardon, and then receives God's assurance of forgiveness. The church brings prayerful petitions and expresses faith that God will hear them.

To worship, as the Bible sees it, is to give yourself up, body and soul, to another. You present yourself, prostrate yourself, lay yourself out before someone else, offering to that person all that you are and all that you have.

You do this from a conviction that the other person *deserves* such unconditional surrender and that it's therefore fitting for you to offer it. Bowing and kneeling are the age-old emblems of this surrender.

"O come, let us worship and bow down, let us kneel before the LORD, our Maker! For he is our God."

Answering this call to worship is a counter-cultural, almost subversive act because much contemporary culture thinks it is humiliating to surrender to God. To worship God, to confess our failures and assign life's blessings to God, to praise and thank God with massed and adoring voices — to take this posture is so undemocratic! That's one reason why secularists, especially humanists, are offended by the sight of people on their knees.

Sad to say, some Christians have become uneasy too. In a consumer society, churches sometimes convert Christian worship into a religious variety hour that focuses not on God but on us and on what makes us tingle. God then becomes our "gofer," whose job is to make us rich or happy or religiously excited or filled with self-esteem.

These maneuvers are not counter-cultural but counter-scriptural. To the writers of Scripture, the beginning of wisdom — and the beginning of worship — is the fear of the Lord. The fear of the Lord is a mixture of awe and love, a dreadful love that knows, as C. S. Lewis once put it, that God is good but not safe. Like Aslan in *The Lion, the Witch, and the Wardrobe,* God is "good and terrible at the same time."

That is why God-fearing people not only exult in the Lord, but also bow down before him.

> *Give us, O God, humility to accept your greatness, awe*
> *to acknowledge your holiness, and gratitude to adore*
> *your goodness, through Jesus Christ our Lord. Amen.*

What Does the Institutional Church Do?

112

*[Paul] continued speaking until midnight. A young
man named Eutychus, who was sitting in the window,
began to sink off into a deep sleep while Paul talked still
longer. Overcome by sleep, he fell to the ground three
floors below and was picked up dead.*

ACTS 20:7, 9

Christians identify with figures in the Bible: Strong people identify
with Samson, wise ones with Solomon, tall ones with Saul, and short
ones with Bildad the Shuhite. Many of us identify with Eutychus, who
began to sink off into a deep sleep while Paul "talked still longer." For
any of us who has fallen asleep during a sermon, Eutychus is our man.
He knew no souls are saved after twenty minutes.

Preaching is proclamation of God's Word. Preaching is an official
task of the institutional church and a mark of any *true* church. By a
preacher's interpretation of God's ancient Word, God himself may
speak to us again today. There is something old in preaching: a biblical
word is read and explained. But there is also something new: that word
is particularly directed to us here and now — to *these* people at *this*
time and place. A good sermon, as Karl Barth said, is prepared by a
preacher who has one eye on the Bible and the other on the newspaper.

Questions about the Church

A sermon has failed if after hearing it anyone could reasonably ask, "So what?" An effective sermon will lay forceful claim on us, demand clear response from us. It will be preached so deeply into our lives — into our guilt and our longings, our moral puzzlement and frustration, our fresh fears and fragile hopes — that we will leave church with two ideas running powerfully through our minds: "What a great God!" and "What a great hope we now have!"

Let's admit it doesn't always work out that way. Those of us who are preachers sometimes manage no better than to thrash around among conflicting ideas and feelings. Or we get fascinated with matters that are truly uninteresting to the rest of the congregation. Or we belabor what is painfully obvious. Some of us preach at great length, supposing we may never see these people again. How right we are. Meanwhile, we who listen set up the Eutychian defense: We begin to nod as if in agreement and gradually fall dead asleep. Some sermons, after all, do pack great sedative power.

The church today needs not less preaching, but better preaching. It also needs better listening. The two go together.

Could it be that Paul and Eutychus owed *each other* an apology?

> *Your word, O Lord, made the heavens. Your counsel stands forever, and the thoughts of your heart are our salvation. Amen.*
> — FROM PSALM 33

What Does the Institutional Church Do?

113

As often as you eat this bread and drink the cup, you proclaim the Lord's death until he comes.

1 CORINTHIANS 11:26

When you were buried with him in baptism, you were also raised with him.

COLOSSIANS 2:12

Thomas Howard has pointed out that we often show how important a thing is to us by "acting it out." We perform a ritual. We not only say something; we also do something that says something. Thus, in one ritual two people approach each other, extending their right hands. Then, taking hold, the two people pump their locked hands rapidly up and down through a six-inch vertical plane. They *shake hands,* of all things! Wordlessly, their ritual says "Hello!" or "Nice to meet you!" or "Congratulations!" or "It's agreed, then!" Sometimes people say the words out loud at the same time their hands are shaking. It's a kind of hand-mouth coordination.

While some rituals accompany events that keep happening, other rituals celebrate a past historical event of great significance: We set off

Questions about the Church

fireworks to recall a declaration of independence; we carve a turkey and eat a bountiful meal to remember ancestors.

Sacraments, or ordinances, do both: They celebrate historical events as well as ongoing reality. With certain words and acts we celebrate memorially our Lord's great acts: He once gave his body and blood for us; he once went down into death and came back up into life. Now by the Lord's Supper and baptism we not only remember these events; we also "act them out." We reenact them with the "signs" of breaking bread, pouring wine, dipping in water. With words and with ritual acts we say to God and to ourselves: "We are the people of these Christ-events and of all that they mean."

But, strangely and wonderfully, the very reenactment of these past events becomes for us a means of *present* grace. For by our breaking, eating, pouring, drinking, submerging, and washing, God himself acts here and now to refresh us for the way ahead. By giving us ritual gifts and letting us use them, God says he is our gracious God. By receiving these gifts, we say we are God's grateful people.

The faithful administration of the sacred rituals is a main task of the institutional church and a mark of any *true* church. By these present ritual acts, we align ourselves with what Christ did in the past and are nourished for what he will do through us in the future. In other words, baptism and the Lord's Supper unite us to Jesus Christ — the same yesterday, today, and forever.

O Lord God, in your mercy supply us for the way ahead. Remind us that we are your people, that we are the people formed by Jesus Christ, your Son and our Lord. Amen.

What Does the Institutional Church Do?

114

*For myself, I feel certain that you . . . have real Chris-
tian character and experience, and that you are capable
of keeping each other on the right road.*

ROMANS 15:14 (PHILLIPS)

Some Christians have old, and somewhat uneasy, memories of the
exercise of church discipline. They remember the terrible drama of
"silent censure," the ominous public mention of a name, the embarrassment of meeting the offender, the hushed atmosphere in a congregation when excommunication occurred.

Churches are doing less and less of this cracking the whip over the
backs of straying sheep. It's mostly because erring sheep amble out of
range. They simply leave the fold. Or join some other flock. They
don't care about our church discipline. As far as they are concerned,
we may read our forms and go through our procedures as much as we
like. They will just fly out of our orbit.

Church discipline is an official task of the institutional church
and a mark of any true church. It must not be neglected. But neither
must it be seen too narrowly. We have long thought of church discipline as merely official — something that only church officers could

Questions about the Church

do. We have thought of it as the pressure brought to bear on an offender by a church council.

But church discipline is not mainly what church officers do to us; it's what we do for each other. The point is to help each other become better disciples of Jesus Christ. Disciplining is a kind of discipling that includes mutual teaching, admonishing, leading, helping. Very often it is *encouraging!* In essence, church discipline is a matter of "keeping each other on the right road."

When children in our church are baptized or dedicated, we promise to receive these children in love, pray for them, help care for their instruction in the faith, and encourage and sustain them in the fellowship of believers.

We vow to help keep them "on the right road," to include these growing children of God in a nourishing network of accountability. Seen in this way, church discipline is not a threat but a *promise.*

You, O God, have sent redemption to your people. You have commanded your covenant forever. Holy and awesome is your name. Through Jesus Christ our Lord, Amen.

— FROM PSALM 111

What Does the Institutional Church Do?

115

You will receive power when the Holy Spirit has come
upon you; and you will be my witnesses in Jerusalem,
in all Judea and Samaria, and to the ends of the earth.

ACTS 1:8

In the past the church regarded its world missionaries as a team of its best and bravest Christian soldiers. World missionaries were an elite corps of shock troops. Before they dispersed to their lonesome and difficult work, the Christians at home prayed with them, spoke encouragement to them, and assured them of their continued interest and support. When these troops returned home from Japan, Nigeria, Argentina, or the Philippines, they were warmly and gratefully received. Naturally, we were glad to hear about their work and see pictures of it.

Some parts of the church show signs of a dangerous shift. Some church members can't even name their own missionaries. They don't know about them or care about them. When missionaries return, they are greeted with mild interest and a request to keep their program short. Some missionaries who offer to report about their work are told that it's not necessary. Missionaries who don't fit into the foreign culture to which they were called return home to discover they don't fit into their "home" culture either. It can be deeply discouraging.

Questions about the Church

A lapse of interest in missions is a sign of decay in the church. Let's confess the truth: A church that doesn't extend itself and doesn't *care* to extend itself is diseased. A healthy Christian church is always reaching, witnessing, adding on those who are being saved.

The institutional church does mission work, international and domestic. The extraordinary people who do this work represent Jesus Christ. But they also represent us. We must know their names, write them letters, pray for them with our children, deliberately take an interest in what they are doing. In fact, in our neighborhoods and workplaces, *we* ought to do missions.

For without mission obedience to Jesus Christ, the church will dwindle and then it will begin to die.

O Lord, we confess that we know more about movies than missions. We have neglected those who represent us in speaking the gospel in faraway places. Forgive us, we pray. And stir us to follow their work, carried on across the world. In Jesus' name, Amen.

What Does the Institutional Church Do?

Question 24

How Is the Church
Related to the State
and the Kingdom of God?

We can't quit meditating on the church without saying at least a word about two relationships of the church with entities outside itself. One of these is the state; the other, the kingdom of God. It should not surprise us that these are both political *entities, given that the Bible has much to say about our relationship to God and to the rest of creation in political terms. King, kingdom, Lord, sovereignty, and many other biblical terms express patterns of authority and obedience that have become the basis of whole systems of theology oriented to the "sovereignty of God."*

The relationships between church and state, and between church and kingdom, are complex. Still, at a sort of ABC level, we may ask, How is the Christian church related to the state and to the kingdom of God?

116

Let every person be subject to the governing authorities;
for there is no authority except from God, and those
authorities that exist have been instituted by God. Pay
to all what is due them — taxes to whom taxes are due,
revenue to whom revenue is due, respect to whom re-
spect is due, honor to whom honor is due.

ROMANS 13:1, 7

Robert Hudnut once recalled one of President William Howard Taft's favorite stories. It concerned a man who had to give a dinner speech on the topic, "The Christian in Politics."

> Well [said the president], the fellow rose at the invitation of the toastmaster, gazed out over the expectant audience, bowed and commenced. "Mr. Chairman, ladies and gentlemen. I was assigned the topic for tonight's dinner, 'The Christian in politics.' I did a great deal of research on the subject. I turned over half-a-dozen libraries. And my conclusion is simply this. There ain't no such thing."

(The Sleeping Giant)

Questions about the Church

Sad to say, this cynic has his descendants in the church today. For them, politics and religion don't mix. Church and state are like fire and water. The state is a necessary evil in a brutal world and it's best left to brutal people to manage as they see fit. Meanwhile, the church's task is to save souls and dispense "spiritual" blessings — a safe concern for preachers, children, and other innocent folk. Hitler's spinmeister Joseph Goebbels said, "Let the churches serve God; we serve the people."

This is demonic propaganda. Christians may never abandon political power to the sons and daughters of this world. Why? Because, as Abraham Kuyper said, over every square inch of human existence, Jesus Christ says: "This is Mine!" Christ is Lord over all; biblical Christians are therefore *political* Christians, called to participate in the ongoing reformation of the state.

Part of our political responsibility is obedience. So long as the state does not order what is contrary to the Word of God, we obey it as a divine institution. We obey even silly rulers and inconvenient rules. We pay taxes. But we also do more: we vote. We run for office. We lobby and petition. We try to encourage justice and discourage injustice. We pray for judges, lawmakers, and executives.

That is, we do everything in our power as the church to give the state what it has coming from us. We "pay our dues," rendering to Caesar the things that are Caesar's and to God the things that are God's.

Your word is upright, O God. You love righteousness and justice. The earth is full of your steadfast love. Through Jesus Christ our Lord, Amen.

— FROM PSALM 33

How Is the Church Related to the State and the Kingdom of God?

117

Then he said to them, "Whose head is this, and whose
title?" They answered, "The emperor's." Then he said to
them, "Give therefore to the emperor the things that are
the emperor's, and to God the things that are God's."

MATTHEW 22:20-21

A published hymn offers stirring stanzas. The words are strong. They
are colorful. They are deeply reverent. Listen.

> Washed in the blood of the brave and the blooming,
> Snatched from the altars of insolent foes . . .
> Vainly the prophets of Baal would rend it,
> Vainly his worshippers pray for its fall;
> Thousands have died for it, millions defend it,
> Emblem of justice and mercy to all.

(Liberty)

What is the object of this high praise? What is being venerated in
these breathless words? Salvation through Jesus Christ? The church?
The gospel? The holy Bible?

Questions about the Church

None of these. The last stanza shows its true colors: "God bless the flag and its loyal defenders. . . ."

The flag! This is a hymn to the American flag!

Of course patriotism is a good thing. During national emergencies it can hold a nation together. We don't like to hear citizens of a free country speak with malice toward their own land any more than we like to hear them speak that way toward their school or their mother.

But there is a deadly idolatry here for Christians who get their love for country confused with their love for God. These Christians want to sing national anthems at hymn-sings, fly national flags in church sanctuaries, identify "the Way" with the American Way, and obey the government no matter what it tells us to do!

Against this sort of temptation it may help some of us to remember the reign of terror and murder that accompanied nationalistic idolatry in Hitler's Germany. It should help all of us to recall that one day our Lord took a coin in hand and used it to make a distinction between the things that are Caesar's and the things that are God's.

Someone once put it neatly. Caesar's coin had Caesar's image on it and belonged to Caesar. We have God's image on us and belong to him.

We must never get these images mixed up.

Loving God, thank you for national gifts and freedoms. Thank you even more that we belong to you and to your Christ. From all civil religion, deliver us; for all true religion, preserve us. Through Jesus Christ our Lord. Amen.

How Is the Church Related to the State and the Kingdom of God?

118

> *Therefore, O king, may my counsel be acceptable to you: atone for your sins with righteousness, and your iniquities with mercy to the oppressed, so that your prosperity may be prolonged.*
>
> DANIEL 4:27

The Christian church obeys the state, but obeys God first. The state is God's instrument of justice and peace, but, like all else, it needs reform. So we offer obedience, but not reverence. We honor the state, and also keep an eye on it. Sometimes we honor the state by protesting its evil, and by refusing to give in to it. After all, Caesar is emperor, but Christ is Lord, and Christians are people who know the difference.

The Old Testament prophets were pioneers in protest against injustice. Knowing both God's righteousness and a nation's unrighteousness, a daring prophet such as Daniel would stand squarely before a king and tell him the truth about justice and mercy, sometimes paying a heavy cost for his bravery.

Since then, ordinary people of God have found themselves called to give similar witness. Armando Valladares spent twenty years in Fidel Castro's prison system. He had protested oppression, and then he had refused political "rehabilitation." So Castro jailed him. But

Questions about the Church

Valladares, a strong Catholic, was a believer in God, and so were some of his fellow prisoners. They never quit protesting evil, even when their protest meant they would suffer more evil. They cheered each other's courage. They kept each other sane. They went on 36-day hunger strikes to protest beatings, rotten food, and naked incarceration in absolutely bare concrete cells. They smuggled information out of prison, tried to escape, and reproved their guards ("How can you beat us like this and then go home and hug your daughter?"). Above all, they simply refused to capitulate to Cuba's dictator. They *would* not bow to him, or wear his blue uniform, or enter his program of political rehabilitation.

A number of the prisoners were bayoneted or shot; many died of malnutrition or of pneumonia. But they kept their faith that Christ was Lord, not Castro, and eventually their witness reached the world through the memoirs of Armando Valladares.

> *O magnify the* LORD *with me, and let us exalt his name*
> *together. Taste and see that the* LORD *is good; happy are*
> *those who take refuge in him.*
>
> — FROM PSALM 34

How Is the Church Related to the State and the Kingdom of God?

119

Then comes the end, when [Christ] hands over the
kingdom to God the Father, after he has destroyed every
ruler and every authority and power. When all things
are subjected to him, then the Son himself will also be
subjected to the one who put all things in subjection
under him, so that God may be all in all.

1 CORINTHIANS 15:24, 28

Toddlers sometimes play with nesting boxes that fit inside each other: one box fits inside a bigger one, which, in turn, fits inside a still bigger one, and so on. All the boxes fit into the biggest one.

In Scripture, the highest, widest, deepest reality is the kingdom of God. It's the biggest box. Into it fits everything God has made, and under it lies everything we have made — all our groupings, associations, relations, structures. In fact, the kingdom includes not only *what* God rules, but also the ruling itself. "Kingdom" suggests both realm and reign, both domain and dominion.

The kingdom of God is the sphere of God's sovereignty — namely, the whole universe. In the vivid imagery of Isaiah 66:1, heaven is "God's throne" and the earth is "God's footstool." God is *God*, after all, the author of galaxies, the redeemer of all the earth, the "King of kings and Lord of lords."

How does the church fit in? The church is an instrument of God's ruling. God uses the church to proclaim the reconciling events of Jesus Christ; to bring about this reconciliation by preaching, disciplining, praying, forgiving; and to embody the reconciliation in its own life as a restored people who love each other, pray for each other, work with each other. In this way the church becomes a test model of the final perfection of God's people.

Let's admit that talk of the kingdom often becomes theological jargon — the kind of talk that puzzles people or bores them. Perhaps we do best, then, simply to pray what Jesus taught us: "Our Father in heaven, your kingdom come." At once Jesus spelled out what he meant. "Your kingdom come" means "your will be done on earth as it is in heaven."

On earth the church is the primary instrument of God's will.

Our Father in heaven, your kingdom come; your will be done on earth as it is in heaven. In Jesus' name, Amen.

How Is the Church Related to the State and the Kingdom of God?

120

I tell you, you are Peter, and on this rock I will build my church, and the gates of Hades will not prevail against it. I will give you the keys of the kingdom of heaven, and whatever you bind on earth will be bound in heaven, and whatever you loose on earth will be loosed in heaven.

MATTHEW 16:18-19

The Fall left a terrible mess. God's cleanup is now happening not only inside the church, but also outside it. God has ways and means beyond the scope of God's people. This is a dimension of God's universal sovereignty and a part of the lordship of his Christ. God's rule extends even to the depths of hell and the outposts of atheism and the farthest reaches of space.

But on earth, God's people are his primary instrument. They are not just one among many, but the *main* tool in God's kingdom. Thus, in the medical field, God's people work not for prestige, but rather for the satisfaction of following their Savior, who hated disease and often cured it. In business and industry, God's people work not merely to amass capital but deliberately to provide goods and services that enable other creatures of God to live better. In education, God's people

Questions about the Church

seek not merely to stimulate and satisfy intellectual curiosity but also to deepen their knowledge of God and God's world, so as to become better servants of both. After all, Jesus commanded us to love God with all our *mind*. Then he sent disciples out, commanding them to teach everything he had taught them.

The people of God have since become a flourishing organism, variously organized to do law, business, medicine, education, science, and the arts in a way that retakes a part of creation formerly lost to the enemy. Here the church is the body of Christ, moving across the kingdom, reclaiming old ground, refurbishing a tarnished creation.

But within this people of God is also the institutional church. It too is not just one Christian institution among many; it's the central institution. For it has been entrusted with the "keys of the kingdom." Through its corporate life, people may become models, witnesses, and agents of the kingdom of God. These are large keys. And they open to us a reality of incredible greatness and wonder.

> *All your works shall give thanks to you, O LORD, and all your faithful shall bless you. They shall speak of the glory of your kingdom and tell of your mighty deeds. In Jesus' name, Amen.*
> — FROM PSALM 145

How Is the Church Related to the State and the Kingdom of God?

Questions about the Last Things

How Do We
Face the Future?

We turn, finally, to the "last things." We have asked questions about God and humanity, and about Jesus Christ, who unites them. We have asked about salvation and about the Christian church, noticing that the church is not an add-on to the gospel of salvation, but a part of it.

According to Scripture, the church is on its way toward the end of history, when the kingdom of God will come in all its fullness. What may we expect at the end? If God plans some last things in the story, what sorts of things might they be? Indeed, how do we face our own "last thing" — our death?

The final meditations address such questions. We begin by asking about our general perspective as Christians in facing what lies ahead: How and where do we set our hope?

121

He who rescued us from so deadly a peril will continue
to rescue us; on him we have set our hope that he will
rescue us again.

2 CORINTHIANS 1:10

One of the cruelest of Christian illusions is the belief that the biblical saints were always saintly. Take Paul. Didn't he stand chin-deep in trouble and shout that nothing can separate us from the love of God? Didn't he sing even in prison? Didn't he declare that we are "more than conquerors through him who loved us"?

He did. Paul knew how to blow the trumpet for God, and how poor we would be without the sound of it. But in today's passage we discover that Paul has known some of the same discouragement that troubles the rest of us. In fact, as he puts it, "We were so utterly, unbearably crushed that we despaired of life itself" (2 Cor. 1:8).

No flags fly in this verse, and it's a comfort to some of us who know what Paul is talking about. We know the feeling that life is demanding from us far more than we can give. We know what it's like to be paralyzed by grief or fear.

Paul talks of despair — the bottom of the soul and the essence of hell. Over the gates of hell, so Dante writes, are these words: "Abandon

Questions about the Last Things

all hope, you who enter here." Put off hope. And put on despair forever and ever.

Against such hopelessness Christians throw every weapon God provides, including "the encouragement of the Scriptures" and "the power of the Holy Spirit" (Rom. 15:4, 13). From the Word and the Spirit, we know that God may be trusted to keep his promises. God has delivered us before; he will do it again. The knowledge of God's triumphs in history helps us because our hope arises not just from dreaming dreams and seeing visions — not just from looking ahead, but also from looking back. As the historian Christopher Lasch has written, hope arises as much from memory as from anticipation.

To a Christian this means that hope springs from the Exodus and the resurrection. Hope springs from Ascension and Pentecost. So Paul, who has met Jesus Christ in the wilderness, stares despair in the face, sets his face toward the future, and speaks hope to us and the whole Christian church:

> He who rescued us from so deadly a peril will continue to rescue us; on him we have set our hope that he will rescue us again.

> *O God, we hope for what we do not see and we wait for it, but the wait is long. Rescue us, O God. In your mercy, rescue us again. Through Jesus Christ our Lord, Amen.*

122

We also boast in our sufferings, knowing that suffering produces endurance, and endurance produces character, and character produces hope, and hope does not disappoint us, because God's love has been poured into our hearts through the Holy Spirit that has been given to us.

ROMANS 5:3-5

Certain Christians in the Middle Ages thought of despair as a kind of folly. But optimism can be just as foolish, and only counterfeiters try to pass it off as Christian hope.

Some people are born optimists. They seem to have been born sunny-side up. They whistle at seven in the morning, enraging everyone in their car pool. They smile pleasantly during tax audits. They are naturally upbeat. Their motto, someone has said, is "Don't worry! It may not happen."

Fair enough. But let's not confuse optimism with biblical hope. Optimism says, "Don't worry! It may not happen." Hope says, "It may happen. But God will keep us." Optimism says, "Things will become better." Hope says, "By God's grace *we* will become better, and better able to deal with trouble." Optimism says, "Cheer up." Hope says, "*Look* up. Your redemption is drawing near."

Questions about the Last Things

Christian hope comes to us as a gift in the wilderness. It's "faith on tiptoe," straining toward a future that has to be faced realistically. Like Abraham, Christians sometimes don't know where they're going, but they "hope against hope" and soldier on. Sheer endurance of this kind produces good character, says Paul, and good character produces hope.

But let's be frank. Many of the things we hope for never arrive. We hope for excellent health, and get fourteen years of chronic fatigue syndrome. We hope for marriage to a particular person, but he marries somebody else. We hope for stable faith, good friends, and a yard full of azaleas in the spring. We hope to be respected by our peers and to go down to our graves full of years and full of gratitude.

Some of these things never come. Most of us have our share of trembling hopes, faint hopes, dashed hopes. A novelist once said that "to live is to bury some hopes." We've all done some of this burying, sometimes quite a while after our hopes were dead.

Yet, in this graveyard, Christians grasp the one hope that "does not disappoint us." As Paul knew, Christian hope grasps the risen Jesus Christ. In fact, Christian hope rises *with* Jesus Christ, the one whose love can restart a dead heart.

> To you, O Lord, we cling. Rise above our sorrow, above our fear, far above our despair. Rise and draw us up through your rising, by the power of your great love. Amen.

How Do We Face the Future?

123

*Why are you cast down, O my soul, and why are you
disquieted within me? Hope in God; for I shall again
praise him, my help and my God.*

PSALM 43:5

NBC once reported on a woman who had taken assertiveness training. She was so impressed with what she had learned that she decided to help those who still lacked this sharp new tool. So she set up a commercial service called *Assertion*. People could call her and hire an asserter to do their asserting for them. And it worked! People called! Some wanted to ask for a raise but didn't want to do the asking themselves. Others wanted anonymously to inform their friends of their breath quality. A few wanted *Assertion* to complain to neighbors about the noise level of their parties.

For a time the woman and her staff were busy and happy. They helped all kinds of people make their desires known and their demands understood. All over town, people enjoyed higher wages, sweeter breath, and quieter neighborhoods.

But then things changed. One woman wanted *Assertion* to call her husband's company and tell them he was manic-depressive. A number of customers asked the staff to write insulting letters to selected

Questions about the Last Things

friends and strangers. Several asked the *Assertion* staff to call them back and talk dirty to them.

Eventually the founder of the company gave up and got an unlisted number. She had hoped to help others. But her hope had gotten lost in the sheer perversity of human nature, which is famous for turning hope to disillusionment.

Sad stories of this kind remind us of a central biblical truth — one that we relearn again and again. Our help is in the name of the *Lord.* So is our hope. And the Lord often raises up hope when our own hopes have just died. Outside Jesus Christ, disillusionment can curdle into cynicism. In Christ, disillusionment can become the seed of new life. How often God plants hope in the soft soil of a sadder, but wiser, heart!

So the psalmists cry from the depths to a guilty and weary people: O Israel, hope in God. And sometimes, deep calling to deep, a psalmist addresses his own soul with a word of life:

"Why are you cast down, O my soul, and why are you disquieted within me? Hope in God; for I shall again praise him, my help and my God."

> *Vindicate me, O God, and deliver me! O send out your light and your truth; let them lead me, let them bring me to your holy hill and to your dwelling, O God, my God. Amen.*
>
> — FROM PSALM 43

How Do We Face the Future?

124

For to this end we toil and struggle, because we have our hope set on the living God, who is the Savior of all people, especially of those who believe.

1 TIMOTHY 4:10

When medical scientists want to test the effectiveness of a new drug, they divide patients into two groups, injecting one group with the new drug and the other group with a placebo — an inactive substance used only as a "control," or basis of comparison, in the experiment.

Scientists are pleased when the new drug helps some of the patients. But sometimes they discover that the placebo helps a number of people too — some of them quite dramatically. Why would an inactive substance make people feel better? Why the "placebo effect"? The reason, according to Karl Menninger, is that the people receiving the placebo have been injected with hope, one of the most active substances known to humanity.

"Where there is life there is hope," says Becky Sharp in *Vanity Fair*. Conversely, where there is no hope, there is no life — at least not for long.

Victor Frankl confirms this with his report of life in a concentration camp. Frankl tells of fellow prisoners whose hope of release began to wither. They reached a state of almost complete apathy. They would lie in their bunks, refusing to answer roll call or go out on a rock squad. The threat of a beating, the prospect of being shot — none of it would get them up and on their feet.

Then, in 1944, word got around that the war would be over by Christmas. Tired men, dangerously sick men, struggled to their feet and attempted their tasks with a new light in their eyes. Some of them even laughed for the first time in months.

But Christmas came and went. The war went on. And in the week after Christmas, prisoners died like flies. No epidemic raged. Conditions got no worse. There was simply a loss of hope.

We need hope to live. And we need hope in Jesus Christ to live eternally. The kind of godliness that attaches to Christ in faith, hope, and love is the kind that "holds promise for both the present life and the life to come." Remarkably, those who have hoped most confidently for the next life have often lived most exuberantly in this one.

Why? Because they believe the war may be over soon?

No. They believe that the war is already over. As Karl Barth wrote, Easter is "the proclamation of a victory already won. The war is at an end — even though here and there troops are still shooting, because they have not yet heard the news."

To this end we toil and strive, O living God, because we have our hope set on you and on your Christ. In his name, Amen.

How Do We Face the Future?

125

Blessed be the God and Father of our Lord Jesus Christ!
By his great mercy he has given us a new birth into a
living hope through the resurrection of Jesus Christ
from the dead.

1 PETER 1:3

Victor Frankl wrote of men who died from lack of hope. Irina Ratushinskaya tells of men and women who lived off hope. In her book entitled *Grey is the Color of Hope,* she tells a remarkable story of prisoners who not only survived captivity, but also walked out of captivity stronger than when they walked in.

Irina Ratushinskaya spent four miserable years in a Soviet prison camp as a state criminal. Her crime was writing poetry that certain officials disliked. One day some of them came to make her pay. She had never known what it meant to "leave everything and follow Jesus." She hadn't known what it was to have everything stripped away, including her own toothbrush. Or to go to sleep without knowing whether tomorrow you would be killed.

Most of us can imagine numbness, fear, resentment. But Irina Ratushinskaya's overwhelming emotion was a sense of security, of which she writes matter-of-factly. Security, not fear. Security, not hate.

Questions about the Last Things

She discovered that it's not only wrong to hate one's captors. It's also foolish. People who let themselves hate their captors start to die. The first thing that happens is that they can't sleep. The second is that they can't eat or digest. Eventually, they destroy themselves from the inside out.

What Irina did was to develop a special bond with her captors. She prayed for them. She spoke gently to them. She prepared herself to witness for them at the final judgment. In the fourth century, a church father wrote that those who suffer will get special "pull" in heaven. They will stand before the judgment seat and identify their tormentors, but then they will say: "O Lord, I forgive him. I put my wing over him." And the Lord will honor this request. In fact, the Lord will encourage all victims to forgive their tormentors, so that the victims may learn the ways of God.

A new birth into a living hope through the resurrection of Jesus Christ from the dead! In a verse for the Easter vesper service, the Albanian Orthodox Prayer Book concludes with these lines:

"Resurrection Day! Let us embrace one another. Let us call brethren even those who hate us. Let us forgive all wrongs on Easter Day, and let us exclaim:

> *Now Christ is risen in glory, trampling down death by death,*
> *and unto all the dead he gave life again.*
> *Now Christ is risen in glory, trampling down death by death,*
> *and unto all the dead he gave life again.*
> *Now Christ is risen in glory, trampling down death by death,*
> *and unto all the dead he gave life again.*
> *Amen!*"

How Do We Face the Future?

Question 26

How Do We Face Death?

Hample and Marshall's Children's Letters to God *includes a few simple sentences about death from a young boy: "What is it like when you die? Nobody will tell me. I just want to know; I don't want to do it."*

Most people don't want to die. They fight to live. But they are curious about this question of the ages: "What is it like when you die?" They think nobody tells because nobody knows.

Yet followers of the resurrected Jesus Christ know at least something about death. The following meditations will engage us not only in what we know but also in how we should practice what we know. We take up a powerful and sensitive question: How do we face death?

126

The living know that they will die.

ECCLESIASTES 9:5

Until about 1970, Western society tried to keep a secret. The secret was that we all will die. Till the avalanche of "death and dying" literature buried it, a conspiracy of silence surrounded human death. And many of us still belong to the conspiracy.

So we avoid the words *dying, death,* and *dead.* We don't say, "He died." We say, "He passed away." Life insurance brochures have often been especially careful: "If anything should happen to you. . . ." (Like what? Like inheriting a million dollars?) In some cases relatives have tried to get a person to decline and die without her even noticing. Physicians don't like to tell the sober truth to terminal patients. Funeral cosmetologists present dead bodies in the position of someone taking a nap. I appreciate these signs of kindness and respect. But they also help keep the secret. A Boston minister reports that relatives of a dead person once objected to his reading the Twenty-third Psalm at the funeral on the grounds that it contained the word *death.* These relatives knew a funeral was no time to raise *that* subject!

But even through our silence, we know the truth. "The living know that they will die," the Preacher says.

Questions about the Last Things

At any rate, once people get past age forty they know it. Someone has suggested that early in their forties most people psychologically try on their shroud. It's a farewell to innocence. You know that when your parents die, you move to the head of the line. As you grow still older, the conclusion is eventually unmistakable. Your friends die, one by precious one, and you know that you too are very mortal. The streets toward death are all one way. And you have already been traveling for some time.

Even children travel these streets. Researchers have observed that even some apparently innocent children's games and songs have an old and eerie significance:

Ring around the rosies,
Pocket full of posies,
Ashes! Ashes!
We all fall down!

A dying unbeliever once asked for "terminal candor." No Christian will face death the way he did — as a wall rather than a door. But the candor we can use. Unless our Lord returns first, we will all die. We will all fall down. And we all know it.

> *O God, our help in ages past, our hope for years to come, our shelter from the stormy blast, and our eternal home. Amen.*
>
> — HYMN WRITTEN BY ISAAC WATTS

How Do We Face Death?

127

For the wages of sin is death.

ROMANS 6:23

One of the Grimms' fairy tales, recalled by William May, is about a young boy who can't *shudder*. He is particularly incapable of shuddering at the sight of death. Instead of recoiling from a corpse he encounters, he attempts to play with it. Deeply ashamed of his son's inability, the boy's father sends him off to shuddering school. Obviously his boy had not yet become fully human if he is so comfortable with death.

The past several decades have seen a death-with-dignity movement that has at least something to recommend it — terminal candor, for instance. Be honest with dying people, says this movement. Tell people what ails them and call the disease by its right name. Don't isolate dying people or treat them like things without human and civil rights.

So far so good.

But, in spite of themselves, many of the "let there be death" enthusiasts still detour around the truth. They suggest that death is just a part of life, that it's "natural," that it's indeed a sort of chum. Formerly, only stoic philosophers and English romantic poets talked of death as a kind friend. Now secularized Americans do it too. In a brilliant arti-

Questions about the Last Things

cle on "The Indignity of 'Death with Dignity,'" Paul Ramsey once wrote that the same program that gave us "calisthenic sexuality' also promotes "calisthenic dying." For some, dying has become an exotic art. Dying is as chic as ballet. The idea is to train yourself to flutter gracefully to your end, like the star of *Swan Lake*. You die with style. You die without inconveniencing anyone. You die *"pianissimo."*

People who think like this need to learn how to shudder. One place to send them would be to the Bible. The Bible does not see death as natural, or as a kind friend, but as an *enemy* — "the last enemy to be destroyed" (1 Cor. 15:26). Ecclesiastes says there is "a time to be born and a time to die." And in cases of tragedy or of extreme old age, death can come as a relief. Still, death in the Bible is an alien, an intruder, a prime misery of our fallenness. Human death is something that *should never have happened.*

Death is the wage sin pays and, without Christ, it is the last indignity.

> *Loving God, we can't face death alone, and we can't face it as those who have no hope. Now attach us to Christ, who is the pioneer not only of our faith but also of the way through death. In Christ's name, Amen.*

How Do We Face Death?

128

For the wages of sin is death, but the free gift of God is eternal life in Christ Jesus our Lord.

ROMANS 6:23

The Bible presents two main teachings about death. One is that death is an enemy. The other is that because of the mighty work of Jesus Christ, death for a Christian is a *conquered* enemy.

Death is an enemy, even though ancient and contemporary pagans deny it. Death, they say, is a graceful and natural free-fall from the tree of life. Like an autumn leaf we ripen and finally twirl to the ground. The beauty of death!

But surely we know this is contrary both to the clear teaching of Scripture and to all clear-eyed experience. Death is always a separation; often it's a painful ripping and tearing. Sometimes a dying person suffers; almost always, those left behind suffer too. They experience grief that feels like fear, terrible emptiness, and sometimes self-reproach. Then for years they remain vulnerable. An aroma, a discovered hat, a snapshot or videotape — these things can reawaken the sense of loss so that we need to be comforted all over again.

When Lazarus died, Jesus did not sing a praise chorus. Jesus wept. He grieved. And when our Lord turned to face his own death, he acted

Questions about the Last Things

not with stoic calm and quiet resignation, but with struggle, revulsion, and prayers for reprieve. Jesus Christ *hated death like sin*.

Jesus wept. Then he called Lazarus out of the tomb. Jesus suffered under Pontius Pilate, was crucified, dead, and buried. Then God called *him* out of the tomb. Death could not hold him. God led Jesus clear through death to the other side.

The women who came to Jesus' tomb, says G. K. Chesterton, found that their Lord was alive; it was *death* that had died in the night! For all of us who are moving twenty-four hours a day toward our deaths, there is one truth, one bittersweet truth to be grasped and held. Death is an enemy, but — thanks be to God who gives us the victory — it is a *conquered* enemy. Weeping may stay for the night, but joy comes with the morning. "The wages of sin is death, but the free gift of God is eternal life in Christ Jesus our Lord."

Thanks to you, O Lord, for your unspeakable gift.
Amen.

How Do We Face Death?

129

He himself likewise shared [flesh and blood], so that through death he might destroy the one who has the power of death, that is, the devil, and free those who all their lives were held in slavery by the fear of death.

HEBREWS 2:14-15

Douglas Nelson retells the sequel to the story of Lazarus — a sequel that comes from an early Christian tradition. The legend is that after Lazarus was brought back to life, he was asked about his experience in the interim. People begged him to tell what he had seen or heard in the life beyond the grave. Had he seen angels? A white light at the end of a tunnel? The risen Lord himself? But Lazarus didn't reply. Instead, very quietly and very joyously, Lazarus laughed.

It's only a legend. But the laughter is medicine for what ails us when we face death. We Christians know about eternal life. We have heard of joy in the morning. We believe Jesus Christ has conquered death. We really do. And yet, we are *afraid*. Fear of death, as Hebrews says, can enslave us not only when we are about to die but also for a whole lifetime.

We are afraid of dying — of operations and chemotherapy, of suffering and helplessness, of pain and paraphernalia. We are afraid of

Questions about the Last Things

becoming a burden. We fear losing our independence and self-control. We are afraid of losing those we love and of losing our *life*, which, in all of its difficulties, can often be so sweet and good. Some of us are afraid of meeting God, who knows every shabby thought that has ever crossed our minds.

Yet we must die — and not as those who have no hope. Someone has compared a Christian's dying to a child's movement down a flight of stairs to a basement. It's late. There's an emergency and the lights have all gone out. From the basement the child hears her mother calling to her. The child can't see anything. She is thoroughly afraid. She doesn't want to descend those stairs. She doesn't know what's there.

Yet she knows *who's* there. And so, perfect love casting out fear, the child moves toward her waiting mother.

Even for God's children death is a valley of shadows and darkness. But, as Richard Baxter put it, "Christ leads me through no darker rooms than he went through before." And in that darkness it's not God but death that comes as a stranger. The one who stands beyond death will be the loving God for whom we have been longing all these years.

> *Dear Lord, it's only when we see the valley of shadows that we look to the hills whence our help comes. It's only when we fear death that we see life, in Jesus Christ, Amen.*

How Do We Face Death?

130

So teach us to count our days that we may gain a wise heart.

PSALM 90:12

We will die, and we will try to meet death with faith and hope. But, meanwhile, how should we *live*? How should we live "toward death"?

Paul Ramsey mentions two responses to the knowledge that we will die. Hedonists apply their hearts to eating, drinking, and being merry — for tomorrow they die. That's the response of people so earnest about their pleasure that you wonder how much joy they actually get out of it.

The other response is from those who know they are held by the everlasting love of God, not only in this life but also in the life to come. These are Christians who have resolved to live fully but not frantically. These are people who number their days so as to get a *wise heart*.

The numbering of our days begins when the "sense of transience" awakens. It becomes instantly more precise when we come back from a brush with death. One of the people who survived an incredible "death-dive" of a passenger airliner over Michigan later said how much each new day meant to him. Colors were more vivid, smells more savory, music and laughter more delightful.

Questions about the Last Things

So it is. So every day should be for Christians who believe they have been rescued from eternal death and will be guided through physical death. We may count our days, reckoning each one as a gift. With deepening wisdom, we may see which things really matter. As someone has observed, when the Day of Judgment arrives, the Lord is unlikely to say to any of us, "I do wish you had spent more time at the office."

For Christians, human life is not a waiting game or a spectator sport. We are given our days as a gift from God, who intends us to use them well. Sloth, or laziness, used to be thought a deadly sin. People don't ordinarily find it so deadly any longer. But it is. It's a premature death. To spend life waiting, drifting, watching television, playing cards, killing time, is a waste of a precious natural resource.

Admittedly, some Christians drive themselves wild trying to achieve. But many others go down to their graves early in life and lie there, waiting for death to come. They never even *try* to live the lives God gave them.

"So teach us to count our days that we may gain a wise heart."

> *O Lord, support us all the day long, until the shadows lengthen and the evening comes, and the busy world is hushed, and the fever of life is over and our work is done. Then, in your mercy, grant us a safe lodging, and a holy rest, and peace at the last; through Jesus Christ our Lord. Amen.*
>
> — FROM THE PRESBYTERIAN WORSHIPBOOK

How Do We Face Death?

Question 27

What about
the Consummation?

We come, now, to the end. This last group of meditations deals with the attitudes, events, and final things that attend the end of history. One day our Lord will bring history to its telos, *its goal. The Lord will* consummate *history. A number of important questions surround our belief in this. We end by asking them under the general question: What about the consummation?*

131

Therefore, keep awake — for you do not know when the master of the house will come, in the evening, or at midnight, or at cockcrow, or at dawn, or else he may find you asleep when he comes suddenly.

MARK 13:35-36

But know this: if the owner of the house had known at what hour the thief was coming, he would not have let his house be broken into. You also must be ready, for the Son of Man is coming at an unexpected hour.

LUKE 12:39-40

The Second Coming has always held a particular fascination for certain Christians. Here they are — Christians with their charts and graphs, their Bible prophecies and pocket calculators, trying to figure the day and the hour of our Lord's return. Some have made confident predictions, including not only the time but also the *place* Jesus has chosen to land. So far they have always found it necessary to revise his schedule.

It's not as if the fact of our Lord's return is in doubt. As Anthony

Questions about the Last Things

Hoekema has pointed out, the New Testament ripples with certainty about Jesus' reappearance. The theme is sounded one way or another in every one of its books. But the New Testament — indeed, our Lord himself — tells us that we will not know the time. In fact, it's none of our business. Our task is rather to *watch*. Stay alert! Be on the lookout for the unexpected Lord!

The images for his coming are remarkable: He is both a householder and also a household thief! The Son of Man is like a householder who comes home suddenly and catches his servants in bed. Or, incredibly, the everlasting Son of God is like a thief who comes silently in the night.

What's the point? Of course, the thief has good reason not to announce his coming; he wants his visit to be a surprise. He doesn't want you to go to the trouble of preparing a welcoming party. He doesn't want you to fuss.

Is that it then? Does the sudden God delight in catching us off guard? Is he like a parole officer who makes surprise calls on his clients? Is he like an employer who spot checks what's on your computer screen?

No. The point is not that our Lord hopes to catch us napping. Just the opposite. He hopes to catch us wide awake, on the job, eager, expectant. Readiness is all.

Yet Jesus' prediction is that we will be surprised. He will come when we least expect him.

Perhaps one day when we are in church?

Come, thou long-expected Jesus, born to set thy people free; from our fears and sins release us; let us find our rest in thee. Amen.

— HYMN WRITTEN BY CHARLES WESLEY

What about the Consummation?

132

*The Lord Jesus [shall be] revealed from heaven with his
mighty angels in flaming fire, inflicting vengeance on
those who do not know God. [He will be] marveled at
on that day among all who have believed.*

2 THESSALONIANS 1:7-8, 10

In one of his sermons, Wallace Alston retells a story by the great Dane,
Søren Kierkegaard. Kierkegaard describes a theater in which a large
crowd was attending a play. When a fire started backstage, an actor
rushed upstage to shout a warning to the crowd: "The theater is on
fire! Get out!"

But the people did not get out. They nodded and giggled and
stayed right where they were.

The actor became desperate. He gestured and shouted louder. He
pleaded with the people to believe him. And the people were impressed. Truly this was a fine actor. They rose to their feet and began to
applaud!

Alston wonders whether the end of the world might come in the
same way — prophets urgently announcing it and people applauding
their act.

One of our profound problems is that we see so little. We can't see

Questions about the Last Things

God. We can't see heaven or the things of heaven. We can't even see much of what God is doing in our world. We walk by faith, not by sight. And, to be honest, our faith often fails to grasp the reality of what it confesses. Up against the daily realities of traffic congestion and market reports, the things of faith can seem airy and remote — such things as dreams are made of. Thus, when preachers gesture and shout and plead about these things, we feel like congratulating them! What a rendition! What a performance!

But one day we will see and hear a stirring and commotion *outside*. Jesus Christ will return with power, fire, and the hosts of heaven. The play will be over. The lights will come on, and we will be confronted not just by a solitary Lord but by a whole heavenly community! An invasion. A whole new world — "something," says C. S. Lewis, "it never entered your head to conceive."

In this invasion each believer will experience a moment of terrible beauty and recognition, a moment to stammer: "I have heard about this day, but I *never* thought. . . . I had heard of you by the hearing of the ear, but now my eye *sees* you."

> *Beautiful Savior, Lord of the nations! Son of God and Son of Man! Glory and honor, praise, adoration, now and forevermore be thine! Amen.*
>
> — GERMAN HYMN TRANSLATED BY JOSEPH SEISS

133

When he was at the table with them, he took bread, blessed and broke it, and gave it to them. Then their eyes were opened, and they recognized him; and he vanished from their sight.

LUKE 24:30-31

Peter Eldersveld used to tell the story of Albrecht Dürer's masterwork, *Praying Hands*. At a time when Dürer and a friend were young and struggling artists, the friend generously undertook manual labor to support them both. Gradually his own artistic career faded. Years later Dürer wanted somehow to repay the friend who had sacrificed himself so kindly. At last he decided to paint the hands that had toiled for him — hands stiffened and calloused by years of heavy work. He called his painting simply *Praying Hands,* and those hands have since become famous across the world.

Hands are among God's choicest gifts. Most of us have a brace of hands — a matched pair. They are ingenious tools, capable of extraordinary speed, power, and accuracy. We are reminded of this whenever we hear one of the world's great pianists. But all of us use our hands in countless ways every day. Indeed, some of us who have a particular way with things are "handy."

Questions about the Last Things

Artists have tried to paint our Lord's hands, the hands that once cut boards, healed lepers, blessed children, touched eyes, broke bread, and washed the feet of disciples. Artists have done their best with Jesus' hands, picturing them as strong and sensitive.

But, in fact, all we know about his hands is that at the end they were hammered to a crosspiece by a Roman executioner. One Friday Jesus opened his hands to be wounded for our transgressions and bruised for our iniquities.

The next Sunday two men on the road to Emmaus talked with a stranger about their dead Lord and their dashed hopes. And then, over a small meal in a lamp-lit room, the men were shocked into recognition. "He had been made known to them in the breaking of the bread" (Luke 24:35). A certain turning of the wrist, perhaps, and a movement of the fingers! And, of course, the scars. Like Thomas, these men knew their Lord by his wounds.

Jesus Christ was the first fruit of the resurrection, which is a resurrection of the body. Christians believe in "the resurrection of the body and the life everlasting." An implication is that for all eternity we shall have our hands.

Will we use them? Will we cut boards, swing racquets, play bongos, greet friends? I think so. I think the new heaven and new earth will include vocations as well as vacations. And if Albrecht Dürer's friend is there, perhaps he will take up his paints and brushes and return to his first love.

Raise us up with Christ, O God, and prosper for us the work of our hands. O prosper the work of our hands. Amen.

What about the Consummation?

134

Then the king will say to those at his right hand,
"Come, you that are blessed by my Father, inherit the
kingdom . . . for I was hungry and you gave me food."
. . . Then he will say to those at his left hand, "You that
are accursed, depart from me into the eternal fire . . .
for I was hungry and you gave me no food."

MATTHEW 25:34-35, 41-42

Jesus' parable tells us a day of judgment follows the resurrection of our bodies. We get the impression from this parable that our judge will not ask us first how often we have read the Bible or prayed, how many times we have enjoyed a church service, or how eagerly we cultivated the sort of personal piety that says "Lord, Lord" all the time. Of course these things nourish our faith, but Jesus Christ will want to ask what has *come* from faith. As always, he will judge the tree by its fruits. And by fruits he means good works.

Two sorts of trees — that is, two groups of people — will stand before him. Two groups of surprised people. One group consists of do-gooders. They have graciously welcomed hunger-relief experts and have taken on themselves the same financial burden to relieve hunger as others do to take a luxury vacation. They have adopted or-

Questions about the Last Things

phans, visited prisoners, used their wealth to set up charitable foundations. They have acted politically in the interests of people who lack political muscle. They have spent money, time, emotional energy — they have spent *themselves* — ministering to the least of Jesus Christ's brothers and sisters.

These are people whose level of self-conscious piety may be low. They are thus amazed to hear the kindest words of heaven coming at them: "Come, you that are blessed by my Father, inherit the kingdom. . . ."

And the others? They too are surprised. In fact they are stunned. Their record shows plenty of good works, but all the good deeds seem to have been done for themselves and their friends. The record shows little done for "the least of these."

Here is a parable to rattle every conservative bone in our body. We may try to ignore it or finesse it, but at the end of the day we have to admit that this terrible parable presents a social gospel. In fact, it presents our *Lord's* social gospel, and it therefore ought to sober us. It's true, of course, that all who trust Christ may face judgment without fear. But the parable says this trust is expressed and measured by ministry to the least of these. And by that standard, how many of us can really say we have put our trust in Jesus Christ?

Righteousness and justice are the foundation of your throne, O God. Steadfast love and faithfulness go before you. Happy are those who walk in the light of your countenance. For Jesus' sake. Amen.

— FROM PSALM 89

What about the Consummation?

135

Then I saw a new heaven and a new earth; for the first heaven and the first earth had passed away, and the sea was no more.

REVELATION 21:1

In the great twenty-first chapter of Revelation John shows us what God showed him, namely, an incomparable vision of the homeland toward which the people of God have been moving for centuries. The resurrection of the body allows God's people to inhabit "a new heaven and a new earth." At the beginning we were banished from the Garden, but at the end we will be welcomed to a city — a *garden* city, where rivers flow and the foliage is for "the healing of the nations." Once again "the desert shall blossom as the rose" and "the mountains drop sweet wine." Once again God will look on what he has made and call it "very good." Once again the earth — this earth, renewed — will enjoy unbroken harmony between God, the children of God, and the rest of creation.

John's vision is remarkable not only for what it includes: the urbane riches of technology and culture, the craftsmanship of jewelers and builders, the treasures of nations on parade. John's vision is also remarkable for what it banishes from the City of God. There will be no more tears, no death, no mourning, no crying, no pain. There will be no *night*. Interestingly, there will be no temple. No going to church.

One other thing: The sea will be no more. Douglas Nelson suggests that this may be "one of the most haunting verses in the whole Bible." Perhaps he is right. But what does the verse mean? Why no *sea?*

For John, as for so many other biblical writers, the sea is a symbol of chaos. There it is, stretching out turbulently and mysteriously toward the horizon. This is the home of Leviathan, of the great sea monsters, of the human dead not yet yielded up by the wash and roll of the waters. Strong, restless, heedless of our frailties and needs, the sea reminds us of every chaos that borders human life and threatens to overwhelm it.

And one day the chaos will be gone. Into the disharmony of our world, God will bring harmony. Into our disorder, God's glorious new order. Into our worldliness, God's brave new world. Into our chaos, God's cosmos.

That, for all the ages, is how the story is to end. "For the former things have passed away." But the same Lord who closes the book on this life then turns to open another. For the One who sits on the throne says, "Behold, I make all things new."

> *O Lord, come! Descend to us, we pray. Heal the land and heal the nations. Let your mercies flow now and forever. Amen.*